The MBA Slingshot
for Women

The MBA Slingshot for Women

Using Business School to Catapult Your Career

Nicole M. Lindsay

 PRAEGER

AN IMPRINT OF ABC-CLIO, LLC
Santa Barbara, California • Denver, Colorado • Oxford, England

Library of Congress Cataloging-in-Publication Data

Lindsay, Nicole Marie, 1975-
  The MBA slingshot for women : using business school to catapult your career / Nicole M. Lindsay.
      pages cm
  ISBN 978-1-4408-3152-2 (hardback) — ISBN 978-1-4408-3153-9 (ebook) 1. Master of business administration degree. 2. Women in higher education. 3. Career development. I. Title.
  HF1111.L56 2014
    650.071'1—dc23   2013048510

ISBN: 978-1-4408-3152-2
EISBN: 978-1-4408-3153-9

18 17 16 15 14   1 2 3 4 5

This book is also available on the World Wide Web as an eBook.
Visit www.abc-clio.com for details.

Praeger
An Imprint of ABC-CLIO, LLC

ABC-CLIO, LLC
130 Cremona Drive, P.O. Box 1911
Santa Barbara, California 93116-1911

This book is printed on acid-free paper ∞
Manufactured in the United States of America

To my parents, Thom and Frances McKinney,
who sowed the strong seeds within me

Our deepest fear is not that we are inadequate. Our deepest fear is that we are powerful beyond measure. It is our light, not our darkness, that most frightens us. We ask ourselves, who am I to be brilliant, gorgeous, talented, fabulous? Actually, who are you not to be? You are a child of God. Your playing small doesn't serve the world. There's nothing enlightened about shrinking so that other people won't feel insecure around you. We are all meant to shine, as children do. We were born to make manifest the glory of God that is within us. It's not just in some of us; it's in everyone. And as we let our own light shine, we unconsciously give other people permission to do the same. As we're liberated from our own fear, our presence automatically liberates others.

—Marianne Williamson, *A Return to Love*

Contents

Acknowledgments

The idea for *The MBA Slingshot for Women* began to emerge on an all-ladies trip to Jamaica in February 2011. Within four months, I had quit my job and was working on the book full-time. In the two years that would follow, consulting projects and entrepreneurial endeavors pulled me away, but I kept coming back to it. This journey has been awesome and yet at times challenging. Through it all, I have had the love and support of my husband, Josiah, and I am profoundly grateful for that. Thank you, baby.

I am also grateful for the encouragement and support that I have received from so many of my family members, friends, and colleagues. You all deserve to be mentioned by name, but the list would be too long and I would invariably omit someone important. You know who you are. Now know how much I appreciate you!

A special thanks to Melanie Hart, my bunkmate on that trip to Jamaica, who always pushes me to dream bigger. Thank you also to those who helped me brainstorm, outline, and review chapters and helped me figure out this book-writing business—most notably, Jullien Gordon, Aimee Slater, Chika Anoliefo, Daria Burke, Martin Davidson, Amanda Roberts, Gretchen Anderson, Nadira Hira, Natalie Sullivan, Bonnie Hearn Hill, and Kellie Sauls. A special shout-out goes to my twin brother, Anthony, and big brother, Thomas—just 'cause!

While this book captures much of what I have learned and personally experienced, it was shaped by so many tremendous master of business administration (MBA) women and others I have met along my journey. When I started the interviews for the book, I was headed in a slightly different direction than the one that ultimately got me to *The MBA Slingshot for Women,* but the insights gained were no less valuable. A very special thank you to all who participated in the interview process for sharing your knowledge, stories, and experiences with me: Carolyn Miles, Professor Sherwood Frey, Edie Hunt, Carla Harris, Charisse Conanan, Elissa Ellis Sangster, Peggy Naleppa, Sophia Siskel, Michelle Kedem, Ankur Kumar, Daria Torres, Michelle Haigh, Monisha Kapila, Connie English, Michelle Wonsley, Adrienne Martinez, Mythily Kamath, Margaux Logan, Amy Knapp, Joana Baquero, Laillah Rice, Helen Summers, Nikki Allen, Marsh Pattie, Lauren Nichols, Rhonda Henderson, Katherine Okon, Ruchira Saha, Katherine Shaul, Megan Lesko, and Blair Taylor.

Finally, I want to acknowledge the true heroines of my work, the young women who are embarking on the business school journey. You will hear over and over about the tremendous opportunity that an MBA offers you, and it's true. But remember: the MBA is not the catalyst; you are. You have everything within you to reach your aspirations, and the wind is at your back. Be well.

Introduction

There is much that women can do in business school to close the gender gap in pay, access, and satisfaction. I am a proponent of tackling that which is within our control. We women have a greater role to play in our own success. However, I am not naive, and nor should you be, about the realities of gender in the workplace and in business school.

For a woman to achieve her most audacious career goals, she will need the support of people and organizations around her. And there is ample evidence that such support has not been consistently available. Look at corporate America. Women now make up 46.9 percent of the labor force and 51.5 percent of management, professional, and related occupations, although we only account for 14.3 percent of Fortune 500 executive officers, 16.7 percent of Fortune 500 board of director seats, and a paltry 4.2 percent of Fortune 500 chief executive officers (CEOs).[1] This is indicative of what we also see in government, nonprofit, entrepreneurship, and other industries and professions.

Of the many factors underlying the underrepresentation of women in leadership and our absence from decision-making tables, the most significant are historical, structural, and cultural. As we are all aware, men had a historical head start over women. In 1950, only one in three women worked outside of the home.[2] In 1970, only 6 percent of professional degrees were earned by women.[3] It was not until 1972 that we had the first woman running a Fortune 500 company: Katharine Graham, of the Washington Post Company.[4]

When we did get to the workforce in sufficient numbers, we were met with significant barriers, the proverbial glass ceiling. Corporate cultures and policies that marginalized us have made it incredibly difficult to ascend the ranks of corporate America.

Over the last several decades, we have made progress. Where we were once completely absent, we can now be found succeeding throughout organizations and in some cases leading them. Unfortunately, the progress has been very slow. One might have thought that with the significant increases in educational attainment and workforce participation over the last three decades in particular, we would have seen more women as C-level executives instead of hovering between 3 percent and 4 percent or surely would have no major companies with all-male boards of directors. Instead, almost 10 percent of the Fortune 500 companies have no women on their boards or among their five highest-paid executives. Master of business administration (MBA) programs in most cases have not done much better. Women make up only 14 percent of the governing boards of top business schools.[5]

Business schools, like corporate America, must do more to achieve gender parity. The representation of women in MBA programs is better with women accounting for 36.8 percent of the student body. Female representation in business schools has continued to increase, although it has been slow going. In 2003, women made up 34.5 percent of MBA programs.[6] Unfortunately, business schools have not kept pace with law and medical schools that have already achieved gender parity in their student bodies, with women outnumbering men in some cases.

Women cannot close the gender gap on our own. If we are to accelerate our careers instead of simply enhancing or improving them, corporations need to do more to recruit, retain, and promote us. MBA programs are in the business of preparing their students for business leadership. These students—men and women—are future CEOs. Shouldn't they be educated on gender issues while in business school versus waiting until they are confronted with them when they are leading organizations?

Men have a significant role to play in the advancement of women. The zero-sum gender game—that if women gain, then men lose—is a myth. Increasing the opportunities for us to create value will yield more overall value and a bigger pot of resources to pull from.

While we need help from external sources, it is time for women to take charge of our futures in school and after graduation. We cannot leave our collective destiny to institutions or to our male counterparts to define. They can help, but that dependence got us into the situation we are in now. We did not create the gender disparity, but we sure are exacerbating it. Yes. Collectively, we are enabling it. We are contributing to our lack of advancement, proper compensation, and satisfaction with our professional success.

Women have the talent and the intellectual horsepower to be wildly successful. We have the desire to achieve our ambitious goals. (You know that we like to be large and in charge.) However, we are collectively coming up short in leveraging the talents we possess to achieve the ambitions to which we aspire. We need to turn that around. This book will show you how.

You are heading to business school or on your way in the near future. What is your plan for making the most of your MBA experience? How will you leverage the opportunity to your professional advantage?

On my business school graduation day in 2000, I was on Cloud Nine—giddy with excitement. I was so appreciative of my MBA experience. I was optimistic about my future career prospects. I had been able to access dynamic professional opportunities and was headed to a corporate finance position in Atlanta.

Like so many women before and after me, I had no idea that in spite of all that I had gained, I actually left so much untapped value on the table. I had worked hard in the classroom and in extracurricular activities, yet I had not done the preparation for long-term career success. I had minimized the MBA to a mere stepping-stone instead of the incredible career slingshot that it was intended to be. This was shortsighted, and the results could have been catastrophic.

For three years after I left school and was in the workforce, I dated my future husband Josiah, who was still at the University of Virginia working on his MBA and juris doctor (JD) degrees. This allowed me to stay connected to the school and the community even though I lived 500 miles away. As I chartered my path toward my long-term goals, I became acutely aware that although I had built amazing friendships, I had not developed the requisite professional relationships. I hadn't consciously planned this networking omission, but the absence of those relationships drove me back to school to rectify the situation. Luckily, I had the bridge to campus in order to claim them because I went back to Charlottesville regularly to visit Josiah.

For those three years after my graduation, I stayed connected to the school and the school community and extracted much of the value that I initially left behind. I developed a firm grounding in who I was and who I wanted to become—or what I refer to as ego and aspirations, which we will discuss in Chapters 3 and 4. With this foundation, I then deliberately acquired the knowledge, the skills, and in particular the relationships that would position me for my long-term goals. I developed a strong personal brand that showcased my strengths and capabilities, and I practiced and improved my communication, relationship management, and leadership skills. Leveraging the Darden community, I methodically cultivated my professional network and my cadre of mentors and advisers. At the end of those three years I was on an accelerated path that led to incredible job opportunities, which allowed me to have significant personal and professional impact and strong earning potential, even in the nonprofit sector.

It took me three years beyond business school to get this value from my MBA degree. You can get it while you are in business school so that you don't have to try to re-create the MBA opportunities later. You can take full advantage of your MBA resources and channels to propel you toward your professional aspirations.

1

The Trash Collector
The Power of the MBA

"If you want to be a trash collector, be a trash collector, but be an educated one."

As a former admissions officer, one of my biggest pet peeves is business school application essays that start with famous quotations. I have read thousands of these essays in the last 10 years, and the famous quote lead still irks me, perhaps because it reminds me of my own essays in high school. Back then, I thought that I was incredibly profound citing obscure platitudes that I didn't quite understand. I soon learned that when you begin with such a lofty observation, you spend much of your own essay trying to live up to it.

"If you want to be a trash collector, be a trash collector, but be an educated one."

Yes, I am starting this chapter with a quote, and although it is not from the likes of Mother Teresa or Nelson Mandela, you have to admit, it's a pretty awesome one. I'm not sure whether to attribute it to Frances McKinney or Thom McKinney, so they get joint credit. Those two, my mom and dad, wanted to instill the importance of education in my brothers and me, so they would often employ the trash-collector quote. Although they said that it would be okay if I wanted to pick up garbage for a living, I am pretty certain that they would have had a conniption if I used my parent-funded education for sanitation work unless I were running the company.

(Tip: I still don't recommend starting your business school essays with a quote.)

In all fairness, my parents were trying to arm us for a world where we would be outsiders, a world where we would be questioned and often underestimated. They believed that education was the great equalizer. Although education might not cure all ills, the tools and credibility developed in school would give us the leverage to compete.

The trash-collector metaphor from my parents captures pretty effectively how most people view graduate business school—that the MBA provides the knowledge, skills, and relationships to be highly competitive in business and related fields. The MBA is the most flexible graduate degree that exists. It can be applied to improving the largest multinational company as well as the smallest local nonprofit. There is ample evidence, in the form of successful alumni, to show how an MBA education can make you a better professional. You can be a brand manager, a banker, an entrepreneur, or the CEO of a sanitation company, and you should expect that you will be a better and more successful brand manager, leader, or entrepreneur with an MBA education.

I can say with confidence that earning an MBA from a top business school can enhance your career. Leveraging your MBA credentials and network and using what you learn will make you better at whatever you do professionally. Who wouldn't want to be better? All things being equal, better is awesome. But it begs the question that every pre-MBA candidate should be asking herself: Is better enough? Is being a better brand manager or a better (insert your professional interest) worth the costs, financial or otherwise, of earning an MBA? Is business school worth potentially more than $100,000 in student loan debt, incurred while having no income for two years?

Before we tackle the matter of whether business school is worth such a significant investment, let's talk about what the MBA offers.

The MBA is the most robust professional development degree that exists, providing you with business knowledge, skills, and relationships to deploy directly in your career. Business school is designed to give you advanced general management acumen framed within an increasingly global economic perspective. Regardless of your future job functions, positions, and industries, the MBA will give you a holistic view of business and organizational management. Unlike some other graduate degrees, the MBA is an applied degree; it will provide you with broad analytical skills and real-world insights for adapting to an ever-changing business environment.

While graduate business programs vary in structure and teaching style, they all provide their students with assets to leverage throughout their careers. The three primary assets, which are the focus of this book, are knowledge, skills, and relationships, and we will look at each one in depth in Chapters 10, 11, and 12. These are not the only assets that you can gain from attending business school. For example, another advantage of the MBA degree is that it is a recognized credential that can enhance your professional brand. It is the distinctive knowledge, skills, and relationships of an MBA education, though, that serve as the foundation for advancing in your career. And it is the distinctive elements of defining who you are, articulating your aspirations, and building your brand that allow you to maximize your MBA slingshot and avert the underwhelming, shortsighted results of using it only as a mere stepping-stone.

MBA KNOWLEDGE

While the word "school" is included in the phrase "business school," the actual education or knowledge gained while there is often the most overlooked part of the MBA experience by pre-MBA candidates. Maybe this is because we often define education too narrowly as the classes that we take and the subjects that we study.

In truth, just about every subject you cover in business school you could study outside of an MBA classroom. Barnes & Noble has an entire section on the core MBA subject areas, including corporate finance, financial accounting, statistics, marketing, operations, organizational behavior, leadership, ethics, strategy, and economics. In fact, if a particular business school struck your fancy, you could buy books written by that school's professors and study the subjects on your own according to their approaches and philosophies. The knowledge that you gain from your MBA education, though, will be much more than theories and concepts that can be read in books. The MBA knowledge that you will develop is much broader than that. It will be based on your classroom experiences and also on the cocurricular activities in which you will participate. For example, if you are interested in the financial markets and in working as a trader, beyond your introductory finance class you might also take a course on derivatives or option pricing. Outside of your course work, you might become a member of a student-run investment fund or participate in your school's sales and trading club.

With just about any post-MBA job you will be in a managerial or midlevel role, so your subject-matter understanding will be critical to your success. The courses that you take in business school and the activities in which you participate will enable you to develop practical knowledge to use when you are on the job.

MBA SKILLS

As I mentioned earlier, the MBA education is applied. The value of the degree goes beyond what you know to what you can do, or your skills. New MBA students may have little MBA knowledge before business school because they previously worked in an unrelated field. However, they will most certainly have the core MBA skills, such as analytical and communication skills. In fact, they couldn't have gotten into a top business school without them.

Business school provides opportunities to strengthen, enhance, and practice the skills you already have. General skills that are particularly well suited for study and development in MBA programs include leadership, teamwork, relationship management, and negotiation. For example, you use negotiating skills in your interactions with others constantly in your everyday life, from agreeing which members of your work team will do which tasks to bargaining with a vendor on the price you will pay for a product. Like most, though, you probably have never studied bargaining and negotiating as a discipline, explored the psychology behind this discipline, or practiced it deliberately to develop it as a strength in your toolbox of skills. Considering the clumsiness that most of us display when making the case to our managers for a salary increase or promotion, you would think we would prioritize becoming more effective negotiators.

There are also certain knowledge-based or technical skills that you may learn for the first time upon entering business school, such as financial modeling or operations and process management. Whether through classroom simulations or hands-on student club experiences, you will foster practical skills that you can apply immediately upon returning to the workforce and as you progress in your career.

MBA RELATIONSHIPS

The old adage "It's not what you know but who you know" was probably written by an MBA alumnus. Business school graduates frequently cite relationships built through the business school network as the most valuable aspect of the MBA, and with good reason. When you join a business school community as a student, you gain access to thousands of alumni from around the world working in diverse professional industries in roles that range from entry-level management positions, such as the ones you seek after business school, to CEOs. You also have access to hundreds of your classmates. These relationships will likely have the most significant impact on your two-year MBA experience and affect you beyond, as many of these people will continue to be in your peer group as you ascend the leadership ladder in your career.

While you are a student, your classmates and the school's alumni will serve as industry insiders and experts you can consult as you build your business acumen. They can also be mentors and advisers who guide you through professional opportunities, such as your summer internship. After you become an alumna, these relationships can evolve in incredible ways. If you have proactively and consciously cultivated your MBA network, you may find:

- Business partners with whom to launch an entrepreneurial endeavor. You may start a business venture and find partners and advisers from your alumni network that can guide and support you.
- Informers to provide you with business ideas or leads. If, for example, you take a business development role, exploring new marketing channels for your company, you might access your alumni network as you are researching different industries and options.
- Customers to buy products and services. If you work in private wealth management after business school managing money for clients, you might use your alumni network to build your customer base, pitching your products and services directly to them or leveraging their networks to access potential clients.
- Talent to hire. You may need to hire in your role, and your alumni network can serve as a tremendous resource for talent sourcing. Or you may be seeking new opportunities and can tap your network for leads.

While you likely have already built significant professional relationships from your previous educational, work, and personal experiences, business school provides a unique forum for initiating and cultivating connections that align with your future aspirations. Your MBA network will be full of like-minded people with whom you have a lot in common, so expect that in addition to the professional connections, many of your classmates will become good friends within your social circle. (You might even find a significant other as I did; more on that later.) While not your motivation for attending business school, the personal relationships that you develop can impact you profoundly in your life and in your career.

MBA RETURN ON INVESTMENT

The MBA assets—knowledge, skills, and relationships—gained from business school are self-evident, but for many women the $100,000 questions still remain unanswered. Is better enough? Are the MBA assets gained to make you better worth the significant cost? In answering these questions, let me first introduce one of the most important business concepts you will ever learn: return on investment (ROI).

ROI is a measure to evaluate the return or profit that you make in relation to the money or resources you invest to obtain that return or profit. Let's say you have a lemon tree in your backyard and you are considering whether to launch a gourmet lemonade stand in your driveway. The ROI would be the profit that you make selling lemonade compared against the cost to generate those sales, including drink ingredients, cups, and your lemonade marketing and sales force. If you can't generate a profit and your ROI is negative, you shouldn't invest. If your ROI is positive, you may decide to invest; however, the return would have to be higher than other investments that you might make, such as selling the lemons as is to another lemonade vendor. If you choose to invest in obtaining your MBA, you must expect that the ROI will be positive and will be higher than the return on another professional credential or the return you could get from investing more resources and effort into your current job and career path.

To calculate your MBA ROI, you need to determine the cost of the investment and the potential benefit gained from it. The cost of an MBA investment will be both financial and nonfinancial. The financial costs are pretty standard. They include the dollars expended to attend business school, such as tuition and fees, books, studying abroad, job-search–related trips, and relationship management opportunities (read: all the fun stuff that's done under the guise of building relationships with your classmates). Additionally, you have the opportunity cost of your salary and benefits, which you will give up for two years. The nonfinancial costs tend to be more unique to each individual, such as the impact on family, volunteer, and personal time and the challenge of merging the things that matter to you most with your MBA experience.

While there may be some future costs associated with an MBA, such as maintaining relationships that you built while in business school, most of the costs of the MBA investment are tangible and easy to identify. Calculating your gain from an MBA is a bit more difficult because it requires you to project what will happen in the future.

We just discussed the knowledge, skills, and relationships that you gain from two years in school, so you may be tempted to think of that as the return that you get from an MBA. While there is value in having the MBA credential and assets, the most significant return comes from what you can generate from those assets. As you estimate the value or return that you can get from investing in an MBA, consider (1) the increase in your earning potential (from the relationships, knowledge, and skills); (2) the greater access to management, leadership, and professional opportunities; and (3) the enhancement of personal and professional satisfaction.

Earning potential. Earning potential, the first component of the return on your MBA investment, is a business concept that estimates the largest profit that can be gained from an investment. If a company develops an innovative new product, the company's earning potential may increase significantly based on its prospects of generating more revenue from the new product. Earning potential applies to companies and can be applied to individuals as well. It can even extend beyond the professional realm to very personal considerations.

In my younger (well, single) days, earning potential played a part in my dating life, at least some of the time. I had more than a few conversations with friends about whether our dating prospects had strong earning potential as we assessed their ambition and career prospects. Earning potential was just one factor among many and rarely ranked ahead of good looks. As interesting as it might be to speculate on the earning potential of others, let's instead get back to business and to estimating your earning potential.

In a nutshell, earning potential quantifies your ability to produce and generate value. Consider how, when, and where you produce value and how that enhances and improves people, projects, and organizations. Earning potential is most easily quantified by the salary and benefits that a company is willing to compensate you with or the fee that someone is willing to pay you to provide a product or service. The company or person places a value on what you offer. While it would take some work, we could calculate a value of your skills, knowledge, relationships, and experiences—in part by estimating what they would be worth to others. Earning potential, though, is not simply the compensation that you can demand; earning potential also captures the variety of industries that you can access and the positions that you can secure to make that money. If you are able to add value in multiple ways in multiple industries, your earning potential will be higher than if you can only add value in one way. This is not to say that you will actually make more money but rather that you have the potential to do so—flexibility carries real value because we don't know what the job market will need in the future. The more dollars you can generate in varied settings over a longer period of time, the higher your earning potential will be.

Finally, an often overlooked component of the ROI calculation is the future cost of education if the dream is deferred in your 20s. Many people go back to earn graduate degrees in midlife. There is nothing inherently wrong with this path. Sometimes the additional experience and maturity are necessary for optimal performance in graduate school. Not every young person knows what she wants to do with the rest of her life. But the escalating costs of education cannot be ignored. Do you want to pay two or three times as much for even less ROI, given that a certain number of years will elapse between now and your midlife MBA? Those are years during which the anticipated benefits will not have accrued, so in essence you would be paying more for less.

Greater management, leadership and professional opportunities. Money isn't everything. While your earning potential will be a major input in your MBA ROI, there are other factors to consider, including your access to greater management, leadership, and professional opportunities. There are very few jobs or careers that require an MBA. Unlike in medicine or law, most business roles don't demand specific educational attainment or licensure. With that said, many opportunities are reserved for MBA graduates, particularly in financial services, management consulting, and consumer packaged goods. Desired qualifications for jobs in these areas generally include an MBA; the job description will say "MBA preferred." Organizations value the assets that MBA graduates can bring, and while business school is not the only source for talent, business schools have a glut of candidates who fit the profile.

The MBA facilitates initial access to more substantial management and leadership opportunities, allowing you to get your foot in the door. Once you are inside and in a more influential role, your work can have wider reach and broader impact. Consider the value of what you would achieve with greater access and decision-making authority.

Enhanced personal and professional satisfaction. The third area to consider in estimating your MBA ROI is the enhanced personal and professional satisfaction that you will have. Of the three components of MBA ROI, this is the most nebulous because your satisfaction is completely tied to who you are and what is important to you. You may get tremendous satisfaction from earning the MBA degree because it was a goal you set for yourself. Or you may find greater contentment in earning lots of money, which enables you to pursue other interests or support various causes that are meaningful to you.

Women with MBAs are better equipped to exit and reenter the workforce or to create alternative professional channels. We see this most often in relation to caretaking responsibilities, but the pursuit of happiness and satisfaction certainly plays a part. For many people necessity dictates the actions we take, but there are examples of women MBA graduates making choices largely driven by their desire for enhanced work and life satisfaction.

All ROI calculations, even those estimated by the most sophisticated financial models, are based on inputs that are largely subjective. ROI requires you to project the future, but you can only speculate about what the state of domestic and international economies will be or about what the needs of businesses, nonprofits, and government entities will be. You don't know what your personal situation will be in the future—there will be experiences that profoundly affect your needs and desires and people in your life who impact the roles and responsibilities that you have.

As with any ROI calculation, you must make some assumptions based on comparables, looking at the return that others have obtained after earning their MBA degrees. You can also consider how you have performed and delivered to this point in your career as an indicator of how much you can achieve in the future.

Estimating ROI using the experiences of comparable MBA graduates will likely yield a positive return. The gains in your earning potential, access to opportunities, and satisfaction will exceed the cost of getting your MBA. As you will find out in your first-year finance class, though, even when the numbers work in your favor (a strong ROI), you may still choose not to invest if, for example, the investment does not align with your strategy (in the form of your personal and professional life goals).

The expected MBA ROI has been sufficient to entice women en masse to business school. In 2012, more than 120,000 women took the Graduate Management Admissions Council (GMAT) test, the standardized test required by most MBA programs.[1] But I challenge you to consider whether expecting a positive return from your MBA experience is enough to disrupt your life, quit your job, and go into debt.

The MBA degree has lost a bit of its reputational cache in the last couple of years. This is due in part to shifts to an increasingly global marketplace as well as a tightening of post-MBA job opportunities. Students have a more challenging job-search process and may even have lower compensation than previous graduates as a result of the economic downturn that began in 2007. While these factors should be incorporated, likely causing your MBA ROI to be a little lower, I suspect that your return will still be positive. The downturn was part of the economic cycle of ups and down, and new markets often mean new opportunities. So while the immediate impact is negative, there could be a significant upside in the future.

"*If you want to be a trash collector, be a trash collector, but be an educated one.*" While this is a pretty good mantra for those in secondary and postsecondary schools, its applicability to graduate school comes up a bit short. The trash-collector quote is emblematic of the career-enhancing approach that so many women take to business school—choosing to attend because the ROI is positive and deciding that being better in their careers is enough to justify the investment. In theory, there is no problem with using the MBA as a career-enhancing tool. In reality, though, lots of women MBA graduates got the career-enhancing MBA when what they really wanted was the career-accelerating and life-altering MBA.

It is difficult to differentiate better from the best—career enhancing from career accelerating—which explains why so many women pursue the career-enhancing MBA experience. Consider alumnae from top business schools. They are making more money than before school, they have fancier titles than before school, and they have great friends whom they met in business school (attending business school in one's mid to late 20s with like-minded people equals new best friends). Life is better—MBA women have more than they had before. Unfortunately it is not the best that they could have attained, and frankly it is not enough. I am not suggesting that women should be stockpiling more money and power in a room to plunder Earth! When I say that it is not the best or not enough, this is in reference to the goals and aspirations that those women once had for themselves that they did not achieve or in many cases did not attempt to achieve.

Let me first say that I rarely compare women to men. I don't think that it serves us to constantly compare ourselves to something we will never be. We will never be men, and that is not where our value lies. This comparison requires that we are always focused on what we are not and what we don't have instead of leveraging who we are and what we do have. Also, whether societal or inherent to our gender, we often have different issues than men, child rearing for one. Viewing these issues through a male or gender-neutral lens minimizes their importance.

In this instance I will compare women to men to illustrate where women collectively come up short in maximizing business school to achieve a career-accelerating MBA. On an absolute basis, the return on the MBA investment is quite strong for women, but when evaluated against that of men, we begin to see a gap. In my estimation, women have persistently lower MBA ROI than men. Let's consider the three components of MBA ROI.

- *Earning potential.* The first factor of MBA ROI is earning potential, or a projection of future earnings. However, the gap between men and women MBAs is not a theoretical potential occurrence but instead is a very practical reality. There has been an ongoing national debate about equal pay for women, and we can look to MBA graduating classes for a tangible example of the disparity. Men earn more in their first post-MBA job than women—$4,600 more (comparing men and women with similar backgrounds).[2] And lest you think that this is a negligible sum, over a 40-year career, the typical woman, MBA or not, is estimated to lose $431,000 in pay versus her male counterpart.[3] That pays for a lot of really good vacations, spa days, and maybe one or two college degrees by the time your kids are ready for them. Contrary to popular belief, these differences cannot be chalked up to lower aspirations or having children.[4]

- *Greater access to opportunity.* Men are more likely to start in higher positions after business school than women, even when they have the same profile and experience. It is not an easy road to the top for women.[5] A 2012 Catalyst study on hot jobs found that 18 months after participating in a leadership development program, women were less likely than men to get an international assignment, receive profit and loss responsibility, or have their budget oversight increase by 20 percent or more.[6] A year after completing the program, 51 percent of the men and only 37 percent of the women received a promotion.

- *Satisfaction.* Women's satisfaction with the MBA experience is comparable to that of their male counterparts.[7] However, when considering career satisfaction after business school, a survey of Harvard MBA graduates conducted by the Harvard Business School found that women were less satisfied with their careers than men. "Focusing on men and women younger than 67," the authors of the preliminary findings wrote that "we found that although they place equal importance on meaningful and satisfying work, professional accomplishments, and opportunities for career growth and development, women report significantly less satisfaction than men with each of these aspects of their lives."[8]

Did you have a what-the-heck moment? Yeah, me too. These stats are alarming and are evidence of what I have seen anecdotally in my years since finishing business school. Women MBAs advance in their careers on an absolute basis with the help of their education, but the gender gap still persists. For most, the MBA is a career-enhancing credential but not the accelerator that they intended when they quit their jobs and headed to business school. While there are a number of reasons why women have a lower ROI than men, it starts with us. We are partly to blame for missing out on the career-accelerating MBA experience that we crave.

We began the MBA ROI discussion by quickly outlining the costs that you will expend to get a certain return on your investment. Those costs include such things as tuition, forgone salary for two years, and several nonfinancial costs. While this is an accurate measure of the costs of the MBA to generate a career-enhancing experience, it omits sweat equity, the investment needed for career acceleration. Sweat equity is the effort that you put into building the right knowledge, skills, and relationships consistent with who you are and want to become. The MBA can be an investment with a tremendous return, but the bonus value of an MBA, the career-accelerating value, is only accessed by expending significant sweat equity while in business school. Women are not investing enough sweat equity into their MBA experience, which is yielding a lower MBA ROI.

Too many women are caught in the MBA enhancement trap in which their lives and careers are better than before business school. But women MBAs are not achieving what we set out to do professionally, and we are not happy about it, which is captured in our lower post-MBA satisfaction. I bet that many current MBA students would take offense to my suggestion that collectively they are not leveraging the opportunity or are missing the mark. Women work hard in business school. Add to this that women are more likely than men to come from nontechnical backgrounds and to be younger, and the argument can be made that women are actually working harder in business school than their male counterparts.

Sweat equity, though, is not tied to the number of hours or brute force exerted in the process. Instead, sweat equity in business school drives you to deliberately pursue activities that best position you to accelerate your career and create a slingshot that can catapult you forward.

Taking the MBA slingshot approach enables you to leverage all aspects of the business school experience and exploit it for your career advancement. Will you be more successful if you pursue the career-accelerating MBA slingshot approach over the more laissez-faire career-enhancing approach? Possibly, but we can't be certain. You might get another shot down the road like I did. I underachieved in business school because I didn't understand the importance of MBA sweat equity. My time at the University of Virginia was only career enhancing, but I got lucky. I was able to reach back to the school to develop the skills that I would need to catapult my professional career in nonprofit leadership. I came to fully understand how I could slingshot my career forward. That's what I set out to do, and I did it. After traditional roles in corporate America, I went off in search of my life's work—that which was so tied to who I was and wanted to be that my personal self and professional self were one. I found it, and my impact and personal fulfillment have been immense. The MBA slingshot enabled me to be the transformational leader that I always wanted to be. I delivered results, and I impacted the lives of thousands of young people. I want you to develop your own MBA slingshot to propel you toward your professional goals and tremendous career success.

I got a second chance. You can get it right the first time—with a plan. The good thing about business school is the bad thing about business school. It will offer you countless opportunities—more than you can take advantage of—to build relationships, skills, and knowledge. So what will you prioritize? What will you do to aim your MBA slingshot in the right direction? In fact, what is the right direction for you? What are you shooting for? Not just the job that you want to attain or the career that you want to have but the life that the job or career can help you create. How will you impact other people? How will they experience you? This book will help you find the answers to those questions. It will show you what I learned only later: how to create a career-accelerating MBA experience by actively preparing and executing a plan for business school.

Talk to most MBA alumnae, and they will tell you that they worked hard in school—in the classroom, in activities, and in the job search. What you are also likely to hear is that they did not have a strategy or plan prior to business school to maximize the return on their educational investment by building relationships, accessing the tremendous educational opportunities, and developing critical skills. This was a particularly strong theme that I heard as I interviewed women for this book. They didn't have a plan, and thus their six-figure MBA experience was left largely to chance. Some, like me, got lucky, haphazardly falling into dynamic opportunities, but for such a significant investment, it seems shocking that so many women went to business school without a plan for leveraging the experience. I'm sure you've heard the saying "A failure to plan is a plan to fail."

For most, it's not laziness that drives this lack of focus. We either never think of planning as a must-do action item prior to starting business school, or we erroneously figure that because MBA programs are so structured, everything will fall into place or work itself out once we are on campus. We feel as though we have earned a smooth journey because of the work we put into gaining admission to business school in the first place. Or maybe we are just expecting a miracle. The only miracle here is the one you will make happen—once you have the right approach.

JARGON ALERT

Business school has its own language, and throughout this book, I'll share some of my favorite terminology with you.

C-level. The most senior executive positions in a corporation. The "C" stands for chief and includes the CEO (chief executive officer), the COO (chief operating officer), and all of the other C's.

Due diligence. Preparing for a business deal by researching and analyzing a company or organization. This has become synonymous with any level of research.

Value proposition. The benefits that the customer will receive from a product or service (or advanced college degree) minus the cost of obtaining it.

REVIEW: THE SHORT, SHORT VERSION

- Your MBA will provide you with knowledge, skills, and relationships that you can use in any profession.
- The MBA ROI consists of earning potential, opportunities for advancement, and personal and professional satisfaction. For most women, the business school ROI far exceeds the initial investment.
- Women are getting lower returns on their MBA investments than men are getting.
- Sweat equity, or the effort that you put into building the right knowledge, skills, and relationships consistent with who you are and want to become, enables you to earn a career-accelerating MBA degree.

Ready to start?

2

Ready, Aim, Fire
The MBA Slingshot Approach

A slingshot is a small handheld weapon with a Y-shaped base and a rubber sling attached to the uprights. To fire it, the rubber is drawn back, creating force to catapult ammo in the sling. When used correctly, the slingshot becomes a precision tool able to hit the narrowest target.

Imagine that as you embark on business school, you have an MBA slingshot in the palm of your hand. The base of that slingshot is made up of the business school opportunities that will be available to you. The rubber sling is what turns the slingshot into a powerful weapon and is fortified by the knowledge, skills, and relationships gained in business school. The target is your career aspirations, and you are the ammunition that was designed specifically for that slingshot. When fired, the MBA slingshot will catapult you forward with incredible velocity, nailing the targets that you set.

Business school is the opportunity of a lifetime or, better yet, the opportunity of a career. You will have two years during your MBA program to focus almost exclusively on planning and preparing for the rest of your career. In a job, you are expected to deliver more in terms of work product and effort than you will receive in return in the form of professional development. Business school is the reverse. Of course, you will work very hard, but in return you will obtain game-changing assets that you can use throughout your career. How will business school help you? When you think about the job that you want to have five years from now, maybe business school will help you access the role, getting your foot into a new industry that you might not otherwise be able to reach. Access is important—you can't compete if you aren't even in the game. But I want you to think about how you will be competitive once you are on the job. Consider the expertise, the skills, and the relationships you will need to be successful. Which ones can you build in an MBA program? And how will you develop them once in business school?

ARM YOURSELF TO HIT YOUR TARGET

Discern your true self. To use a weapon effectively, you must ready it by loading it with ammo, aim it, and then fire it to hit the target. The same applies for your MBA slingshot. As you ready your slingshot, your first priority is to discern your true self—present and future—and align your personal brand to that. You want to get clear on who you are and what is important to you (see Chapter 3). This is the foundation that your life and career are built on, so you want it to be strong. Once you have an understanding of where you are now, you then can turn your attention to where you are going. Defining your career aspirations and figuring out who you want to become will enable you set your sights on the right target and point your slingshot in the right direction (see Chapter 4). With greater self-awareness, you are then able to ensure that your behaviors, actions, and personal brand exemplify who you are and what you want (see Chapter 5).

Your MBA slingshot will be fully operational, so once you know the target, you could fire away at it. It is likely, though, that your slingshot is not strong enough to reach your lofty aspirations, so shooting may be futile. Instead, you want to identify specific ways to increase the force of the rubber strip on your slingshot—determining the additional knowledge, skills, and relationships that you will need to hit your target aspirations. There may be industry or functional expertise that you need to develop, skills that you need to master, and door-opening relationships that you need to cultivate to achieve your goals.

Develop your approach to the 4 Cs. With a clear sense of the knowledge, skills, and relationships that you want to develop during your two years of business school, take aim at acquiring them. This is the sweat equity that we discussed in Chapter 1. You will determine the best approach to leveraging your business school channels: the classroom experience, career exploration, club engagement, and community and social life, or the 4 Cs. The 4 Cs frame your MBA experience—any action that you take will be within the context of the 4 Cs. As you define your approach to business school, you can develop your specific plan for each area.

The classroom experience captures your academic goals and course of study (see Chapter 6). Your career exploration is just that—the opportunity for discovery of career paths and options while incorporating the very tangible internship and job search (see Chapter 7). Your club engagement incorporates the activities and leadership roles that you undertake while in school (see Chapter 8). With clubs there will be significant overlap with the other channels, particularly career exploration and also community and social life, which captures the more casual and informal opportunities that you will have to engage in with others in the business school community (see Chapter 9).

These four channels are in place to help you develop your knowledge, skills, and relationships during business school. You will have many options and choices to make—there are trade-offs across the board. By developing an approach that aligns with who you are and who you want to become, you can ensure that you are undertaking those activities that will be most beneficial, not simply following what everyone else is doing. You will only have 24 hours in each day with 168 hours in each week, so defining your plan to leverage the 4 Cs effectively will be critical to your success in business school.

Take action. Planning is critical, but at some point you have to stop preparing and start doing. Fire away! You will put all of the pieces together and take action to build the knowledge (see Chapter 10), skills (see Chapter 11), and relationships (see Chapters 12 and 13) that you need to catapult your career.

While this book is focused on professional success, it is not lost on me that the majority of women who attend business school are single, so I would be remiss if I didn't spend some time talking about dating in business school (see Chapter 14). Dating in business school can impact the effectiveness of your professional MBA slingshot, so we need to address it head-on.

IMPORTANT SAFETY PRACTICES

This book is your MBA slingshot operating manual. And like every other operating manual that exists, before even getting to the product instructions, we must start with important safety practices. These guidelines should be reviewed before reading this book and before wielding your slingshot in business school.

1. Read and understand the instructions before attempting to operate the slingshot. Keep this manual and refer to it regularly. This book provides

information and guidance on properly using your MBA slingshot. Most of the features that you will read about are optional. You will not use them all, and frankly many features cannot be used at the same time. Thus, you must constantly be thinking about what you want and need in order to determine which features work best for your purposes.

2. Be familiar with all of the business school controls and their proper operation. The MBA slingshot is not a complex tool, but it can be maneuvered in many different ways, namely as it relates to the 4 Cs. Consider your options and then approach the 4 Cs deliberately with specific goals in mind.

3. The MBA slingshot is a powerful tool, not a plaything. To operate it, you must be confident that you can maneuver it properly. Even with no previous slingshot experience, anticipate that with study and practice you can effectively operate your MBA slingshot. Don't just trust the tool, trust yourself—you can do it! Through regular usage, you will become more comfortable and highly proficient with the MBA slingshot.

4. Your MBA slingshot is fully assembled and operational. Upon reading these instructions, you can begin to use your MBA slingshot immediately, though acquiring additional knowledge, skills, and relationships will enable you to build a stronger career slingshot.

5. Never allow someone else to operate your MBA slingshot. If someone else must pull a lever or flip a switch, supervise the person closely. You will get well-intentioned guidance, advice, and even direct support from others during business school. This will be tremendously helpful, but at all times you must be in control of your own MBA experience.

6. Only use the prescribed ammunition in the MBA slingshot. You are the ammunition—the sharp, dynamic woman who will pierce your target aspiration. If you use other ammo, your slingshot will fail to operate as intended. To ensure that your ammo isn't a dud, focus on building a strong personal brand, and take great care to determine who you are and what you have to offer.

7. Avoid operating the MBA slingshot without clear targets. Having a target matters! The MBA slingshot is designed to hit specific career targets. While it can be used and frequently reloaded to hit multiple targets or a general area, it is a precision tool. Results may be mixed if you simply shoot in the dark without a visible target. Spend time defining your career aspirations and exploring ways to reach them.

The MBA slingshot is a power tool that can catapult your career. To maximize it, deliberately acquire knowledge, skills, and relationships in business school that (1) align with who you are and (2) position you for who you want to become. The results will be significantly increased earning potential, opportunities for advancement, and the personal and professional satisfaction that you deserve.

JARGON ALERT

Lean in. Facebook COO Sheryl Sandberg wrote the provocative bestseller *Lean In: Women, Work, and the Will to Lead.* She writes that women must "lean in" to their careers and change the way they approach them. (I completely agree!)

Mommy track. A so-called career track that offers benefits such as flexible hours to women with children but usually provides fewer opportunities for getting ahead.

Ready, fire, aim. Business school terminology for what happens when you are in such a hurry to get something going that you forget that you need to aim. For firing to mean anything, we need some plan or direction.

REVIEW: THE SHORT, SHORT VERSION

- Maximize your MBA slingshot by deliberately acquiring knowledge, skills, and relationships in business school that align with who you are and position you for who you want to become.
- Discern your true self—present and future—and align your personal brand to that.
- Determine your approach to leveraging your business school channels—the classroom experience, career exploration, club engagement, and community and social life.
- Take action. Planning is critical, but at some point you have to stop preparing and start doing. Put all of the pieces together and take action to build the knowledge, skills, and relationships necessary to catapult your career.

Leveraging your MBA is not about how someone else succeeded. It is about figuring out who you are, what you want, and the effect you want to have on the world. Those answers will define business school for you. They will help you determine the knowledge, skills, and relationships that are pertinent to your goals.

3

Ego
Discerning Your True Self

Who are you? And who do you want to be? Those are the lofty questions that you actually begin to answer in the application to business school. You may be asked to respond to application essays that, at their core, address these questions, such as "What matters to you most, and why?"—or, what I call the Failure Essay, "Describe a moment in your life that you would live over. What would you change?"

Because business schools want to understand how you will use your MBA in the future, most of their questions tend to focus more on your short-term and long-term professional goals—your aspirations. Good MBA essay writing is primarily about delivering a brief, cohesive story about how you were pretty awesome in the past and how, with the help of business school, you will be even more awesome in the future. So although the essay-writing process challenges you to consider who you are and who you want to be, in most cases you only scratch the surface. MBA admissions teams don't have time to learn everything about you. It is up to you to dig deeper to discover your full aspirations. Before you get to your aspirations, you must first explore your ego.

I don't mean ego in the Freudian sense of the word. Ego is simply who you are. It is the aggregation of all of your parts that total you—a combination of your values, interests, personal attributes, skills, and experiences. Your ego informs the activities, people, and environments that motivate, center, or stress you and is the foundation of your MBA slingshot. Your ego—who you are—determines the launching point to propel you toward your aspirations.

Discerning your ego is a lifelong journey, so don't expect to sit down and in an hour capture it succinctly on one page. The more time you spend considering who you are, reflecting on your life experiences, the more you will discover about yourself.

Your ego, more than your aspirations, will drive how you organically experience business school. For example, if you tend to shut down when facing stressful situations, you might find that the internship recruitment process is more difficult. If you are an introvert, you may find it more challenging to develop relationships beyond your assigned learning team and the two people who sit on either side of you in your section or cohort. If you are aiming to be at the top of your class but tend to be very social, you may become overextended with social events, particularly on school nights. First-year MBA students struggle with these very issues. In most cases, they don't consider how to handle these issues before they start school, so they respond in a reactive way, relying on natural instincts and habits. Instead, you can proactively prepare for the common issues that will arise and act in a way that is consistent with your ego but also with your aspirations.

In discerning your ego, consider the following elements:

- Values are the qualities and beliefs that you hold most deeply. They drive the way you make decisions and guide your daily life. Values develop from your personal experiences, through your education, religion, and other exposure, and they are influenced by your parents and family, friends, and those in your community.

- Interests are the topics, activities, and issues about which you are particularly curious, concerned, or excited. Interests range from a fleeting curiosity about a current event to deep passions that might serve as the basis for your career and life ambitions. My own interest in how people choose their career paths led to my passion for personal development, which ultimately guided me toward running a nonprofit in that area. I knew that I wanted to run a company and be a CEO. I guess another passion of mine is being in charge! Yet although I also wanted to help people with their personal growth, I didn't think about helping people as a career. I was in business school in the late 1990s, so my case studies and models were all corporate. It had never dawned on me that I could find a career in the nonprofit sector. You might be interested in sports, dancing, reading for pleasure, traveling, or working for political causes. Don't dismiss these as simple interests. They may in fact be the foundations of something meaningful. An MBA can support many different passions.

- Personal attributes are the traits and characteristics that make up your personality and differentiate you from every other woman seeking an MBA. They impact behavior and how you interact with others. Your personal attributes, and to some extent your values remain relatively consistent throughout your life. Examples of personal attributes are being hardworking, outgoing, empathetic, patient, and honest.

- Your experiences are the observations or events that shape your world-view and can influence your values, interests, and skills.

DISCOVERING YOUR EGO

There are several tools you can use to discover and articulate who you are. They include self-reflection, assessment tools, feedback from others, and courses, some offered in business school.

Self-reflection. This is the cheapest and most important tool for figuring out who you are. No one knows you better than you. Use self-reflection to consider your feelings, reactions, thoughts, and actions. I tend to be a bit impatient; I want answers quickly so I can move on to the next thing. Over time, I have reluctantly come to understand that self-discovery is a journey that slowly unfolds. I try to take some solace in knowing that today I only know what I know and that tomorrow I'll learn tomorrow's lesson. At least that is what I tell myself!

Consider keeping a journal as you explore your ego. Capture any new insights so you can synthesize them later. I journal on and off. It feels weird to recap my day or something I just thought of. I mean, I just *lived* it, right? In all seriousness, while living daily life, it can be tough to reflect on it in the moment. Writing it down will allow you to revisit your ideas, reflections, or questions when you have time.

Assessment tools and guides. These are just fancy terms for what can be a great starting point in articulating your ego and giving you a framework for your preferences or tendencies. The results may confirm what you already know or may highlight new areas for you to explore, accept, or discard. Even with assessments, you will have to go back through the self-reflection process. Many business schools offer assessments, such as CareerLeader, at no cost to their students, so check with your business school's career services office.

Prescriptive nonfiction titles such as *What Color Is Your Parachute?* can guide you through assessments and exploration of your values, your interests, and your goals. StrengthsFinder is my flavor-of-the-month favorite assessment, partly because anyone can access it (just buy the book from your neighborhood or online bookstore) and you don't need it to be interpreted by someone who is certified in the tool. I also like the philosophy behind StrengthsFinder—that we should figure out our strengths and concentrate most of our energy on them versus focusing on our weaknesses. Makes sense, doesn't it? We have limited time and resources. Let's focus on the areas in which we can be great and change the world! Leave the other stuff to someone else.

I have always been a hard worker, but in my last five years in nonprofit management, I became a complete workaholic in kind of an absurd way—always checking e-mail, working on my days off, and putting in extremely long hours. There were no boundaries; work-life balance was a punch line. For a while I thought I was putting in all of those hours because my team, my organization, and my program participants needed me. As it turned out, the opposite was true. I needed them. When I took the StrengthsFinder assessment, my strongest strengths theme was "significance." Common attributes of people with this theme are that they want their work to be a way of life, want to have free rein over that work, and want to be significant in the eyes of other people. Each of these attributes resonates with me. I am reluctant to admit that I want to be seen as doing important work, but it is true, and without an independent assessment tool I'm not sure that I would have acknowledged that about myself. Assessments won't give you the answers to who you are, but they can give you some powerful clues.

Feedback. Have you seen the famous perceptual illusion of the young girl and the old woman (Internet search: "young girl-old woman illusion")? Can you see both the girl and the old woman? In the FedEx logo, can you see the subliminal arrow? When we look at illusions, it is all about perspective and what our eyes and brain key in on, often ignoring the other alternatives. When defining or articulating our ego, we often do the same thing. We focus on only part of the picture. Gathering the feedback of others can be useful in helping us gain the full view.

Although I really appreciate the insight that I gain when I receive feedback, to be honest I hate the experience. This is true of both positive and constructive feedback; I feel no more comfortable when someone is praising me than when someone is criticizing me. Okay, I feel slightly better when it is positive. I genuinely want to know what I can do better and understand where I didn't meet expectations or achieve my capabilities. In the same way, I want to know what works for other people, what they appreciate about me. Even with all of that, in the moment I don't enjoy receiving feedback.

Several years ago, I had a formal 360-degree review (getting feedback from people on all sides of me, from those who reported to me, my managers, peers, and external sources, clients, and partners). Before I went through this process I was really hard on myself, particularly in regard to my management skills. Before the assessment, I would have said that I wasn't supporting my team enough and that I didn't act in a very measured, deliberate manner, not the way I thought a manager should lead.

The feedback, as it turned out, showed that my style worked well for my team and my organization. From all sides, they trusted me. They felt that I would go to bat for them, that I listened to them, and that I trusted them. They felt that the direction I set was clear. I tell you, this assessment rocked my world! The assessment didn't say I was perfect—it included constructive criticism—but it confirmed a strength that I wasn't sure I had.

I have led with so much more confidence since that assessment. I got validation, and that's what I needed at that point. I needed to know that I could be myself, which is a little silly, pretty laid-back, and still hard-charging when it comes to the work. I valued teamwork and fairness, and my team appreciated and respected that.

It is often said that we grow more from constructive criticism than from praise for the things that we do well. I don't think that's necessarily true. The most significant growth comes from learning both what works and what doesn't work in order to get closer to your authentic and real self. This allows us to gain confidence in who we are and what we do well and recognize areas of development or areas of deficiency in which we need more support or a helping hand.

My 360-degree feedback was formal, but often the most poignant feedback is informal.

A couple of years ago, I had lunch with a former coworker. We had a great time chatting it up and talking about work drama at our old company, which was like a soap opera. Near the end of lunch, she said that she wanted to tell me something (read: unsolicited feedback. I didn't ask for this). She proceeded to tell me that when I joked about people (read: crazy program applicants, some of whom were actually crazy!) with coworkers, it was sometimes offensive and sent the wrong signal to others, particularly junior staff. Damn! She totally deflated my little ego.

First to the feedback and then to the delivery of the feedback. If you spend more than five minutes with me, you will learn that I'm a ham. I love to tell stories and make quips. I don't take myself too seriously—most of the time. I like to make other people laugh at my own expense and sometimes at the expense of others. I'm not one of the Plastics from *Mean Girls,* but I can be a little raw. With my years in admissions, recruiting, and nonprofits, I have read a lot of applications, interviewed hundreds of people, and corresponded with thousands. And let me tell you, people do some bizarre things. I mean, really odd.

When I was making jokes about candidates, I was bringing what I felt was much-needed levity to the office where we worked very hard for little pay, and I had never thought about how my jokes might be perceived—namely that I was ragging on the people we were supposed to be helping. I was doing it in good fun, but it may not have been the right example for the junior staff.

The feedback was difficult to hear; I was definitely taken aback. But I really appreciated my former coworker being willing to give me tough feedback. I listened to what she said and considered how I could incorporate it.

Learn what you do well and what you need to improve from your managers and supervisors as well as from people who aren't required to actually tell you. From whom can you gather formal and informal feedback that will help you discover what you do well and where you can improve?

Business school courses. Now, I hope you are reading this book before business school, but it will help even if you are already there. Business schools, their leadership and organizational behavior professors, and their career management office staffs continue to develop opportunities for students to explore who they are and who they want to become. During my last year in business school, I took a career management course with maybe six other second-year students. Career Management isn't exactly the sexiest course name, but it was an amazing class in which I explored who I was, what I valued, and what motivated me. I could write a whole book about what I learned about myself in that class and how those insights have manifested themselves in my life since then.

The most profound impact of the class was discovering my interest in how people developed professionally and how they reached their goals. The interest was always there, but before that course I didn't recognize that several seemingly disparate activities wove a powerful story. Often our strongest interests are right under our noses, hiding in plain sight. I became aware of my obsession—in a relatively normal way—with understanding people's professional and educational stories. I wanted to know how they got to where they were. It was not simply curiosity; I turned into Barbara Walters probing them. I loved sitting on panels about graduate school and helping prospective candidates navigate the application process as I shared what I had learned.

In my last year of school, I was a graduate adviser to two freshman dorms. Any of these factors could be explained, but taken together, a common thread began to emerge. That year, I first discovered my passion for professional development and the foundation for my life's work. Each of these tools—self-reflection, assessments, feedback, and courses—has helped me, at different times, discern my ego, including my values, interests, attributes, skills, and experiences. As you prepare for business school, think about what makes you tick, what inspires you, what drives you, and what skills and attributes you possess.

As you discover more about who you are, consider how this might impact your MBA experience. You will be in a new environment with the opportunity to catapult you toward your aspirations. You want to act in a way that is consistent with your ego, but you don't want to be completely bound by it. The actions that you take to build knowledge, skills, and relationships in business school should be consistent with your values, interests, and personal attributes. Yet relying solely on your ego may cause you to play it safe—acting in the same ways that you always have. This could severely limit the risks that you take, the people with whom you engage, and the projects that you undertake while in business school. Ultimately, knowing who you are and what is important to you will enable you to make deliberate decisions about your approach to business school with greater awareness of the risks and the rewards.

JARGON ALERT

Bucketizing. Supposedly, an interesting way of describing the process of organizing or putting in categories. Although the term is the object of scorn in the industry, its use is increasing.

Buy-in. A noun that means an agreement or consensus. You need buy-in to make things happen.

Disconnect. Used most commonly in business school as a noun. Inconsistency between what you are saying and what you are doing. Or inconsistency between what you are saying and what I am saying.

REVIEW: THE SHORT, SHORT VERSION

- The search for your true self begins with your ego, a combination of your values, interests, personal attributes, skills, and experiences.
- Your tools to discover your ego include self-reflection; assessment tools; feedback, both formal and informal; and business school courses, even the ones with unsexy names such as "Career Management."

Understanding your ego is the first step toward building your MBA slingshot. The next chapter will deal with the second step: defining your aspirations.

4

Aspirations
More Than an Awesome Job

Ego captures what we already possess. It is the reality of who we are today. Aspirations are what we are striving to attain or become. Many of us women have difficulty defining—let alone articulating—our aspirations. I think that this is because we were conditioned to think about ambitions in the wrong way. From the time we are at a young age, adults around us, well-meaning as they may be, probed us on what job we aspired to have. "What do you want to be when you grow up? A doctor? A lawyer? A writer?" Since our youth, we have been trying to encapsulate, in a word or a phrase, what we want to become professionally. We are deemed ambitious and "so smart" when we can spout off a prestigious profession or role, particularly if it requires lots of education.

Business schools continue this flawed trend, asking what their future students want to be when they grow up as if their applicants are still eight years old. The wording may be a little different. One school asks candidates, "Briefly state your short-term and long-term career objectives. How have your prior professional, academic, and personal experiences influenced your career plans? Specifically, how will your participation in the MBA Program contribute to your career objectives?"

Another school simply asks, "What are your professional objectives?" This is much fancier language aimed at getting a response to the age-old question "What do you want to be when you grow up?" This question draws out an incomplete definition of our aspirations and leaves out the aspects that truly set the course of our lives and careers. To capture the full measure of your aspirations, you must consider *what* you want to be and, more holistically, *who* you want to be. Essay writing for business school application is a good starting point, as you identify the jobs (plural) and the career (singular) that you want to have. Just as or more important, you should also consider the life that you want as well as the impact that you aspire to have on others and on the world.

> Far away, there in the sunshine, are my highest aspirations. . . . I can look up and see their beauty, believe in them, and try to follow where they lead.
>
> Louisa May Alcott

Aspirations, at their highest level, set the course and direction of your life, encompassing both the momentous milestones and destinations to reach and the journey and experiences along the way. As you define your aspirations, you need to consider three aspects: your vision, your mission, and your goals and objectives. Look at any Fortune 500 company or large nonprofit, and you will see that it has a vision, a mission, and objectives that guide how the organization operates, how it makes decisions, and what it stands for. Business school applications in most cases only touch on the third aspect, your objectives or goals, which are more tangible but are far more likely to change than your vision or mission.

Goals not only change repeatedly, but they are difficult to project more than 1 or 2 years out. How many friends do you have who toil over not knowing what they want to do with their lives? Do you? Most of us can't visualize the job that we want to have just 5 years from now; only a few are lucky enough to have that clarity. So it feels nearly impossible to articulate your dream job 10 or 20 years from now. Although long-term goals may be difficult to visualize, I do encourage you to think seriously about them. They, however, are just one aspect of your aspirations. Also consider your vision and mission.

Vision. Your vision captures who you want to be and defines your purpose in terms of your values and highest ideals. Your vision is personal and should be based on your values, those qualities that are most important to you. My vision is just three simple sentences:

1. Be a good steward of my relationships.
2. Do the things I say I will do.
3. Live a simple, fun, and fabulous life.

These are my life principles, my vision for my future. Everything I aspire to links back to this vision. I don't distinguish between home life and work life, because for me they are integrated and frankly seem to merge together even when I don't intend them to. What is the vision that you have for your life? What principles or themes have guided your decisions and actions?

Mission. Once you have set your life direction through your vision in terms of your values, you can drill down to your mission, which defines your purpose in a more tactical way. Your mission captures how you will measure your success and the impact that you want to have.

Remember that Career Management class that I referenced in the last chapter? One of my class projects was a small clay ewer that I decorated at one of those fun pottery painting places. On the ewer—such a cool little crossword puzzle word—I painted "Sow the strong seed." I don't recall the assignment or why my deliverable was an ewer, but today, 13 years later, I still have it, and it still captures my mission to sow the strong seeds that exist in young professionals to help them reach their full potential. It is my belief that we already have everything within us to be successful; it needs only to be cultivated and nurtured. I don't remember how I came up with "Sow the strong seed." It's good, right? The phrase, though, captures the impact that I want to have on the world, to help people achieve their best selves, being all that they can be.

You don't have to develop well-written, succinct statements of your vision and mission. You do need to consider broadly how you want to live, who you want to be, and the impact that you want to have while on this Earth.

Goals. Your vision and mission are the overarching beliefs that guide your goals. I was a little down on goals earlier, so let me clarify. Goals aren't evil. They provide you with critical immediate and intermediate milestones to work toward. Your vision and mission provide a broad foundation, while your goals set the detailed map. There are lots of ways to fulfill your mission and vision, and ultimately the goals you set will capture the specifics—the what, when, who, where, and how of that which you hope to achieve.

For much of my life, I aspired to run a company. The goal lacked specificity—I didn't know the company or the industry it would be in or exactly how I would get there. But it was a long-term ambition, or a destination job.[1] There are so many different ways to attain the top spot in an organization. I could have started an organization and named myself the CEO, or I could have worked in one place and moved up the ranks. Early on, I didn't need to have all of the answers regarding how I would achieve my goal, but I needed a target around which I could frame my more immediate decisions and choices. As I progressed in my career and as my long-term goal became a short-term goal, I needed to map out more clearly how I could attain it.

Ultimately, I chose to build my knowledge, skills, and network through three distinct organizations before taking the executive director position at a fourth employer. My short-term goals in each of those organizations focused less on promotion (because I was comfortable transitioning to another company) and more on building my assets and experiences and delivering results. I certainly didn't achieve every short-term goal that I set for myself. But because they were grounded in my mission and based on my long-term goal, each goal that I attained put me closer to running a nonprofit.

DISCOVER YOUR ASPIRATIONS

You discover your aspirations in many of the same ways that you came to understand your ego in the last chapter—that is, self-reflection, feedback from others, and assessments. As is the case with discerning your ego, feedback from others and assessment tools can be incredibly useful in defining your vision, mission, and goals. My best friend, whom I have known since graduate school, has helped me refine my mission over the years. She has an unwavering belief in my unique purpose and capabilities and is always pushing me when I think too small about my goals. (I wish I could show you a video of her passionately proclaiming what I need to achieve with my life. It's priceless!) She reminds me of my strengths and of those things that are better left to someone else. Having people and particularly women in your network who can serve as encouragers is critical to your success. We'll talk more about this later. For now, as you consider your aspirations, who in your circle of friends can challenge you and also help you dream big?

Getting ideas from others is beneficial, but the process of self-discovery will prove most valuable in defining your aspirations. Only you can determine what is most important to you. Only you can decide the type of person you want to be and what you want to accomplish in your life. Before you can create your vision, mission, and goals, you have to do a little dreaming. Put aside any notions of how you will or will not be able to accomplish your dreams, and unabashedly reflect on the aspirations that are your heart's desire.

Ideally, your MBA application process began with dreaming, but it likely started with pragmatism—determining what you needed to say to convince admissions officers that you were ready for business school. Realistic, reasonable, and foreseeable goals are perfect for admissions essays, but they are not sufficient for ambitious people and leaders. As you embark on the MBA, your realistic goals may be a starting point, but what do you want beyond those? What are your "Big Hairy Audacious Goals" (BHAGs)? For more about that, see Jim Collins's and Jerry Porras's *Built to Last,* a must-read business school book in which the authors assert that companies with unprecedented success have BHAGs. What do you really want? Are there goals, jobs, roles, or opportunities that you can barely imagine for yourself or that you are embarrassed to say aloud? Are there ambitions that you have or once had that you have convinced yourself are unattainable because of some barrier, real or imagined? Is there something you want that feels out of your reach? Do you want to run a business, be a CEO of a multinational company, launch or lead a multimillion-dollar nonprofit, or address an issue or solve a problem facing a market, a community, or a country?

We each have different aspirations that can be categorized as anticipated, realistic, far-reaching, or downright crazy. Only you can determine your aspirations. But make sure that faulty assumptions, fear of failure, or even fear of success are not keeping you from aiming for the downright crazy aspiration. Consider the assumptions that you may be lugging around with the rest of your personal baggage. Is it that you shouldn't try something if you can't be the best and do it perfectly? Or is it that you ought to be planning for marriage and family instead of how to pay for a six-figure education? Be mindful of your fears so you can deliberately decide what you aspire to and consciously combat things that stand in your way.

Your fears and assumptions can have a profound impact on the vision, mission, and goals that you pursue in your life and also on what you never attempt. You may not achieve every ambition that you have, but it is a shame if you pretend that the ambition doesn't exist at all. Then you will never have a shot at reaching it.

The MBA, combined with your professional and educational experiences (with a little career recruiting), will put you on track to attain what are considered realistic post-MBA jobs. You've got the goods. You're smart enough (basic intelligence), competent enough (business and management foundation), and skilled enough (sufficient interview and networking prowess) to land a role. This should give you a lot of confidence as you begin business school. The question that you must consider is whether those realistic goals are really enough for you. Do they capture who you want to be?

Give yourself some time for reflection. Try these two exercises to help you put down that heavy baggage and listen to the inner you. The dying reflection will help you with vision, and the retirement speech will help you with your mission. No one wants to think about getting old or dying, but if we can propel ourselves into the future and consider that which we believe will be most important to us, then we can determine how to let those beliefs and desires guide our lives today.

Vision exercise: Dying reflection. You are lying in a bed, and on this day you will close your eyes for the last time. You will die later today. Look around your bedroom slowly. Notice what fixtures are in the room—the decor and the furniture. Now turn your attention to the nightstands. Are there photographs or get-well cards placed on them? Who is in the pictures? Who sent the cards? Are you alone, or is someone sitting in the room with you? As you reflect on your life, will it be a solitary reflection, or will you share it aloud to another person? As you think back over the years, what are you most proud of? Not necessarily the accomplishments or successes, but how you lived your life, how you interacted with other people, and what you most valued. What lessons would you want to impart on those generations coming after you?

Mission exercise: Retirement speech. Okay, you're no longer dying, just retiring. I'm sure you're happy to hear that. Instead, it is 30 years from today. The retirement party has been planned for you just as you would want—the right size, people, food, and decorations. Consider who will speak during the program. Will there be multiple speakers or just one person? What will the speakers say about you? And when it is your turn, what events, people, places, and ideas will you share with the audience?

GOAL-SETTING TIPS

Articulate true goals. As you articulate your vision and mission, defining your specific and actionable goals will be much easier. Most of us have experience in setting goals, whether related to health and fitness, career, or our personal lives. As you develop your goals for business school and beyond, I challenge you to differentiate between your true goals, which you are willing to make incredible sacrifice to attain, and your wish list, which would be cool to do but if it doesn't happen won't have you lying on your deathbed with regret that you didn't pursue it.

One of my goals is to build a platform that allows me to help thousands of people achieve their potential. I work toward this goal daily. Alternatively, making lots of money is on my wish list—not $1 million or $2 million but $10 million or $20 million. I could have so much fun with that kind of money. In reality, though, above a certain level of comfortable living, making money is not really a goal of mine (much to my husband's chagrin). It is not something that I am willing to work daily to attain. If it happens it happens, but making millions of dollars, although this would be nice to have, is not a true goal of mine. Still, if you have a money-making business idea, don't hesitate to call me!

Don't compromise. I implore you to consider your personal aspirations and your professional aspirations without compromise. Do your goals include having a spouse or significant other and children? Many women do. You can admit it (at least to yourself; you don't have to tell me). If you want to have a family someday, that's great. Don't feel as if acknowledging this somehow makes you less ambitious or less serious about your professional career. I have found that with some young women who do want to have a family this dominates their personal and professional goal setting. Many 20-something and 30-something women I talk with feel an incredible urgency to expedite their careers and relationships so they can have it all, whatever that is. They have lofty career ambitions on the one hand and familial desires, such as marriage and children, on the other. Many feel conflicted, as if they have to choose one over the other or limit their near-term goals to accommodate their long-term ones.

Consider what you want now, and don't begin to compromise on your aspirations before you have a decision to make. There may be a time for compromise, but now is not it. Don't compromise your career aspirations, selecting a job because you think it will lead to a career that is family-friendly, when today you don't have a husband or even prospects for a husband and have no children. Avoid the false sense of urgency. Your biological clock does not sound like a bell in the middle of the town square. An artificial timeline will not serve you well.

Don't let unclear goals derail you. Finally, if your career goals are not completely clear, don't fret. Do the best you can with the information you have now. Don't sit idly waiting for the big aha moment. Waiting for an epiphany about your future could lead to missing out on something that will position you for your as-yet-undetermined long-term goals. My dad likes to say, "Pray with your feet moving." You can hope for perfect clarity, but while waiting on that, do what you can with what you have.

When defining career goals, most people think in terms of what job or industry they would prefer. If you know the specific roles and organizations where you want to work, that's great. If not, keep exploring. While you try to figure out the specifics, continue to focus on who you want to be. What kind of life do you want to live? What impact do you want to have? You don't necessarily have to know the industry in which you want to work in order to determine that you want to run a company, want to manage people, or want to travel the world. In uncovering these ambitions, you, along with others, can begin to conceive of roles or destination jobs that will enable you to fulfill your aspirations.

You will aim your MBA slingshot toward your aspirations, or career targets. The better able you are to articulate your aspirations, the more clearly you can delineate the knowledge, skills, and relationships that will be most advantageous.

JARGON ALERT

Aha moments. Epiphanies of ideas that once discovered seem more like common sense than life-changing revelations.

BHAGs. Big Hairy Audacious Goals. Acronym that you will hear in business school but it just as aptly applied to your personal life. Objectives that capture the full measure of your capability.

Following the herd. Losing sight of your pre–business school career goals and aspirations in favor of the internships that are most popular and pay the highest initial salaries, such as management consulting. Generally occurs in the first semester of business school.

REVIEW: THE SHORT, SHORT VERSION

- Aspirations are more than what you want to be when you grow up. They really deal with who you want to be.
- Aspirations can set the course and direction of your life, encompassing both the momentous milestones and destinations to reach and your journey and experiences along the way.
- The three aspects of aspirations are your vision, mission, and goals/objectives.
- Consider how you want to live, who you want to be, and the impact that you want to have while on Earth. Don't overemphasize a spouse whom you've yet to meet or children who have yet to be born.
- Step out on faith. You can.

Now that you are closer to knowing what you want—for you—from your MBA, you are going to learn how to leverage that with the MBA slingshot and your personal brand.

5

Brawn in Your Brand
Creating a Consistent, Powerful Personal Brand

What do other people think of you? What words would they use to describe you? Would you use those same words to describe yourself? Do people have to get to know you well to be able to figure out what you have to offer? Or do they get a quick sense of what you do well within one conversation? These questions speak to how others perceive you and your personal brand.

Personal brand has been the subject of numerous books. Go online and you will see blogs for the 5 best books on branding, the 7 essentials of a killer brand, the 10 best something or other—you get the idea. There is even a magazine devoted to personal brands. Branding is a popular topic these days, though it was around long before there was a name for it. Although made popular by Tom Peters, it was introduced by Napoleon Hill in 1937. In a time when the concept of self-improvement was still new, imagine what a stretch it must have been for people to wrap their heads around the idea that people should package themselves like a product in the grocery store. That was for toothpaste, soap, and automobiles, wasn't it?

Even today, many people scoff at the concept of personal brand. I understand why people may be turned off by the thought of applying the concept of branding to an individual person. They think of it as creating a fake persona or an alter ego, like pretending to be Catwoman when you are just Selina Kyle or trying to be like David Banner when you are actually the Hulk. You can try to fake it, and that might work on your good days, but on those bad days you quickly revert to who you really are.

Instead of being someone you are not, personal brand helps you more accurately define and authentically reflect who you are. Your brand, which is the sum of who you are, what makes you unique, and how you communicate those two things, drives how others perceive you. This in turn impacts how they regard you, interact with you, and invest in you over time. A strong personal brand can induce others to want to get to know you better personally and professionally. It can enhance your reputation and credibility with others, which enables them to advocate on your behalf. A strong brand allows others to see who you are and what you want so that they know how they can be most helpful to you.

As you develop your MBA slingshot—acquiring the knowledge, skills, and relationships that are aligned with your ego and are aimed toward your aspirations—think of personal brand as the glue that holds it all together. The stronger your brand, the more powerful and sturdy your MBA slingshot will be.

ELEMENTS OF A PERSONAL BRAND

Your personal brand consists of three parts—product, trademark, and marketing—and each is equally important in developing a strong brand. The product that you are showcasing is *you.* It is the sum of all assets that you possess, including your skills, knowledge, experience, values, and principles. On the job, part of your product might be your analytical thinking and ability to solve complex problems. Or in the MBA classroom, your capacity to illuminate marketing concepts based on your professional experiences in the advertising industry might be core to your product. Your product, like that of a company, is the foundation for your brand. If you don't have the goods, you can't build an enduring brand.

Take Apple—maker of MacBook, iPad, and iPhone—which has a killer brand. The strength of its brand is closely tied to the quality and consistency of its products as well as to the customer experience. Apple has faced increasing competition lately but had built its reputation and brand by delivering innovative, high-quality consumer products. Apple invested heavily in product design and development elements that prioritize its customers. An offshoot of this is Apple's in-store customer service division, the Genius Bar, that has become one of the company's trademarks.

Your brand trademark, like Apple's, captures what you do (your results) and how you do it (your style and approach). This is what makes you distinctive and unique. For example, delivering engaging and compelling sales presentations might be a trademark that you have come to display at work. Your personal brand enables other people to connect with who you are. Thus, your trademarks generally will be traits, behaviors, and outcomes that are highly valued and appreciated by others. Essentially, if you alone see value in a trait that you have, it can't be a brand trademark, though it may still be important to you in other ways.

While articulating your product is fairly straightforward, many professionals struggle with defining their trademarks. They wonder what makes them unique. You may find it helpful to ask others what they identify as your trademarks. Look to old recommendation letters and annual performance reviews. Push yourself to identify what makes you distinctive. The more you can differentiate yourself honestly, the more you will stand out. It is what makes you compelling.

You don't have to be the only person of the billions on the planet who has a certain trait or style, but you should be able to find a few things that capture authentically who you are. As you consider your brand trademarks, don't narrowly focus on your professional experiences. You are early in your career, so you may not have worked in professional settings that encouraged you to be completely who you are. In my case, I always seem to find comical or odd aspects in any situation. Humor isn't simply an add-on but instead is a vehicle through which I connect with people. I use it when I facilitate training sessions, lead meetings, and go through my everyday life. Even in the most serious situations, humor is a staple of my approach—it is one of my brand trademarks.

While your product and trademark are the substance of your brand, the marketing is the outward presentation of your brand. Your brand marketing includes every touch point in which you connect to another person. When you talk about your skills in an interview, you are marketing your brand. When your classmates see you arrive 15 minutes late for class every morning, you are also marketing your brand (likely in a negative way).

Marketing often dominates the discussion of personal brand because it is the externally facing element. You can deliberately develop a high-quality product and trademark, but if they aren't marketed well, the strength and reach of your brand beyond those who know you well will be limited. This is often a common theme with women, who tend to be less comfortable with self-promotion and with taking credit for successful outcomes, even when they are the primary orchestrator of those results. While honesty and integrity are important, women also more quickly self-criticize and overstate their responsibility when things don't go well. These behaviors are brand-busting. The way you talk about yourself, your accomplishments, and your failures significantly impacts your personal brand, so you must convey the real story and the greatness of who you are.

KEYS TO A STRONG PERSONAL BRAND

An ideal brand is consistent. It is honest. And it is bigger than you are and exists beyond you. It is your responsibility to build your brand and manage it. Once it becomes viral, though, you will have a more difficult time controlling it. You never know when a YouTube video is going to pick up millions of viewers all over the world. Your brand can go viral as well.

Authentic. When your brand goes viral, you want it to be an accurate reflection of you. A brand is essentially a promise to deliver something with consistency over a long period of time. Your product, trademark, and marketing must be grounded in who you are, not in some fake persona. This is the reason that I wanted you to think about ego and aspirations before reading this chapter. What we call brand is really having knowledge of self and presenting yourself in a way that is consistent with this—knowing what makes you authentically you. It is based on your ego with aspirations mixed in.

Brand is largely intangible. Consider women whom you admire. In addition to possessing skills, knowledge, experience, and unique traits that you respect and value, they likely have that indescribable quality that draws you to them. Like them, you can't control how others, such as a classmate or a hiring manager, experience your brand. But when you interact with them or anyone else who crosses your path in a true and trustworthy manner, they will be drawn to you. They will feel your authenticity, even if they can't put their finger on what is attracting them.

There is nothing that captures the realness that you need in your brand like the word "authenticity"; however, I find this term to be rather passive—just be yourself, and that is enough. This is not quite right. Instead, you should develop a boldly authentic brand. You must genuinely identify what makes you unique and what distinguishes you from your peers in business school and beyond. Why will a company want to hire you? Why will an investor want to commit resources to your business idea? Why will an alumnus want to help you find a job? Remember, that it is based on your product. What makes you awesome? Don't cheat yourself here. Achieving your goals is driven by the confidence that you have that you can actually do it. If you can't articulate traits, values, skills, and experiences that make you fabulously who you are, then you have to go back to the drawing board. This isn't about arrogance but instead is about knowing your self-worth so clearly that it oozes from your pores. Others will be able to sense that you value yourself, and they in turn will be compelled to value you as well.

Aspirational. It may seem a little counterintuitive, but your brand must be authentic (capturing who you are now) and also aspirational (capturing who you want to become; that is, it is not part of who you actually are). It is the aspirational nature of your brand that excites and rallies people around you. When you create a vision of what you can become, others begin to see that in you and then can more readily help you get there. Let's say you aspire to be a CEO. You've never been a CEO—maybe you've never managed anyone directly. It is inauthentic to present yourself as a chief executive; your product and trademark just don't support that. But you can incorporate aspects of personal leadership, sound judgment, and teamwork in your brand that reflect your senior management aspirations. Remember that a brand is not a wish. You need substance and real evidence to back it up.

The trust-building nature of personal brand facilitates relationships. Remember, personal brand is the glue that holds your MBA slingshot together. As others connect with your brand, they become aware of who you are and what you can deliver and also what they can offer to you. Keep this in mind as you consider your business school relationships. Assume that every person you meet can help you in some way. Of course, you won't have time to describe your entire life story and career aspirations to everyone who crosses your path. A strong personal brand, though, will expedite the connection to who you are and who you want to become. As people learn a little about you, based on what you say and do and how you carry yourself, they will be positioned to support you in achieving your aspirations. This could be as simple as sharing a job opportunity, making an introduction to someone else in the community, inviting you to coffee to get to know you, or endorsing you for a campus leadership position.

Consistent. Great brands are enduring. Think about brands that you have come to trust—you know what the product can do and why you choose that brand over others on the market, and you can articulate the brand's value to you. That brand trust and loyalty are likely based on the product quality but more important on its consistency. Your personal brand should foster the same loyalty and commitment from your "customers."

Your business school customers are quite varied and include your classmates, peers, professors, administrators, and school alumni. Your MBA program may also be able to facilitate access to your primary customers, the hiring managers of the companies where you are interested in working after graduation. For each of these customers, consider how they will experience your brand. How do you need to differentiate yourself so that your customers act in the way that you want them to? In what ways should you communicate with them to promote yourself?

While it may be tempting to think about approaching these customers in different ways, you run the risk of having multiple brands that may not be consistent with one another. Inconsistent brands don't grow. They confuse people and breed distrust. Imagine that you have a car that you love. You think that it is the best option at your price point, and it meets all of your needs. Then people around you who have the same brand of car begin to have problems, complaining of issues with the vehicle. Though you have strong personal experience, your trust in the brand may begin to erode. You may be less likely to recommend the brand and may even decide that when you purchase another car, you will consider other brands. This is exactly what happened to Toyota when one of its models had a mechanical issue. The company's brand image took a massive hit, despite the reputation that the company had built over many years for delivering safe and reliable automobiles. Ultimately, an inconsistent brand is far worse than having no brand at all.

PROMOTING YOUR PERSONAL BRAND

The power of a strong personal brand is not just in what you have to offer but is also in how you choose to deliver it. The ways in which you market yourself should be consistent. Marketing is not limited to just what you tell people about your product but also includes conscious and subconscious perceptions of who you are and your capabilities. Remember, every person is not going to have the opportunity to get to know you well. By having consistent presentation, you ensure that no matter when and how someone comes in contact with you, she or he can receive the right messages.

Wear your personal brand. Your attire and appearance are often the first part of your personal brand that others notice. This ranges from the clothes and shoes you are wearing, your cosmetic elements (such as hair, makeup, or visible tattoos), and your behaviors.

Clothes have never really been my thing. I like jeans, and I think that sweatpants are one of the greatest inventions in comfort clothing. But we all know that how you dress impacts how others perceive you and interact with you. When I walk into a room wearing a suit, I am treated very differently than when I have on informal attire. You don't need to wear a suit to school, but consider how your wardrobe supports or detracts from your brand. A challenge for some women in business school is around after-hours attire and how that may affect their personal brand and image.

In business school, there is very little separation between professional life and personal life, so expect that they will largely be merged. You often spend your days and your nights with your classmates. Many women want to get gussied up for the party on a Friday night. But the people at that party will be the same people who are a part of your professional network. Would you wear five-inch heels and a stretch tube miniskirt to a work function? If not (and I really hope not), you might want to put that way in the back of your closet, not to see the light of day while in business school.

Exude your personal brand. You want your brand to be boldly authentic. Others will experience it through your etiquette—for example, how you enter and exit conversations and how you introduce yourself. Your strong nonverbal communication, such as eye contact and the firmness of your handshake, also determine whether others can feel your personal brand in indirect ways. Good posture, for example, may affect how others perceive your confidence and the quality of your brand.

Some measure of swagger is required to exude your personal brand in everything that you do. To be boldly authentic, identify the things that make you feel confident and powerful. You might use a personal mantra that you repeat every morning, such as "I am a leader. I'm fabulous. I'm talented." Say that every day to yourself, and others will feel that sentiment emitting from you. What you say is what you are, and what you believe is what you become. If you don't believe it, you never will be it. If you truly do believe it, you are on your way to making others believe it as well.

Speak your personal brand. The language that you use is important. Be mindful of how you introduce yourself to others. The words that you speak—whether spewing curse words like a sailor, being self-deprecating, or using jargon like an industry geek—impact how others experience your brand. Consider whether your words truly convey the quality of your brand.

Your initial contact and communication with others will not always be face-to-face. In the age of technology, we often build full-fledged friendships and business relationships without ever meeting in person. Electronic communication, namely e-mail and text messaging, has become more common than phone calls and along with social media has blurred the lines on what is private and personal versus public. While navigating this can be tricky, social media provides powerful tools to extend and market your brand, particularly through LinkedIn and Twitter.

A final thought on personal brand. The business school environment can make building a strong brand more difficult. Because your personal and professional lives overlap significantly in business school, you will be visible to your classmates all of the time, particularly as a woman—there are fewer of us there. If you are careless or inconsistent with your brand, this won't go unnoticed. Yet, how can you remain consistent when there are so many opportunities to be experienced, so much fun to be had, and frankly so much more to learn about yourself? Back to your ego. Back to your core values and what is important to you. Even if you haven't decided on every aspect of who you want to be, you know who you are—now. You know what you believe in. If all else fails, let that guide you as you refine and market your personal brand.

JARGON ALERT

At the end of the day. At the end of the day you will tire quickly of this phrase, which means simply "ultimately." The expression probably caught on because of its ring of finality.

Best-in-class. An adjective meaning the best of the best. Frequently used to describe systems, processes, products, and ideas that are the best only in the minds of the creators.

Repurpose. A verb meaning to recycle a process or system and use it for a purpose other than the one for which it was created.

REVIEW: THE SHORT, SHORT VERSION

- Your personal brand consists of three parts—product, trademark, and marketing.
- Your brand product is the sum of all assets that you possess, including your skills, knowledge, experience, values, and principles.
- Your brand trademark captures your results, style, and approach.
- Your brand marketing includes every touch point in which you connect to another person.
- Your personal brand should be authentic, aspirational, and consistent.
- If you don't believe it, you will never be it.

In the next chapter, we will begin our look at the four channels of business school, starting with the classroom experience.

6

Never Too Early
The Slingshot Starts in the Classroom

When we've done something well, it is our natural inclination to repeat it when we later find ourselves in a similar situation. It makes perfect sense—keep doing what works for you. So it goes that if you performed well when you were a student in college, then you can do the same things and expect to do well as a student in graduate school. Use your proven study methods. Engage with your professors to learn the material and get the best grade you can. While there is nothing wrong with how even the best students approach their undergraduate studies, replicating those behaviors will likely cause you to come up short in business school.

Undergraduate students generally study without a sense of professional purpose. There is little regard for integrating their college experiences to serve as the foundation for their career going forward. Truthfully, I'm not sure that 18- and 19-year-olds should be thinking of their undergraduate education in that way, as it may cause them to prematurely focus on a career path without the proper youthful exploration.

Even if you are still exploring, business school will require a much more strategic and deliberate approach if you are to fully maximize it in your career going forward. Over the next four chapters, we will explore the channels, or the 4 Cs, that you will use to maneuver through business school, including your classroom experience, career exploration, club engagement, and community and social life. Alas, the MBA program is two years of school, so it makes sense to start our conversation with the classroom experience.

THE CLASSROOM

No matter where you attend business school, a substantial portion of your MBA program will be spent in a room with four walls, tables or desks and chairs, at least one professor, and a number of fellow students who are there to learn management fundamentals. Every MBA student will study finance, marketing, operations, strategy, leadership or organizational behavior, ethics, statistics or decision analysis, and accounting. While the course names and the structure may be slightly different, the aim is the same—to ensure that you learn the foundations of business.

Because the MBA program lasts for only two years and includes students with varying interests, from management consulting to marketing to investment management and so on, first-year MBA students are challenged to plow through the foundational material at lightning-quick speed. The upside of this is that it allows students to spend their second year, and in some cases part of their first year, pursuing different courses of study to fulfill their specific professional interests. The downside is the pace of learning required to master the concepts. Particularly in the first semester, your classroom experience will be the source of stress. You may feel the pressure and anxiety as early as week one, particularly if you don't have a strong business or quantitative background. I have found that most MBA programs hit their students early and hard with the quantitative course work. By midterms, which in some programs come as early as three or four weeks into the semester, you will certainly feel the crunch on your time and the pressure of sitting for your first set of exams.

EXPLORING THE CLASSROOM MECHANISMS

While the classroom experience will be challenging, it is often the primary source for business knowledge that you will develop, offers a structured setting to build and practice skills, and is the site for initiating and cultivating many MBA relationships. MBA programs are not the same, though. Business schools design their MBA programs differently; thus, your first task in developing your approach to the classroom experience is to determine the structure and learning mechanisms within your program. Even seemingly minor differences can have a significant impact on your experience and the ways in which you should prepare yourself.

Unlocking knowledge. As you consider your approach to your MBA classroom experience, some matters will be very clear. If you are interested in working in human resource consulting, for example, first-year strategy and organizational behavior will be very important courses for your professional development. If you have a particular industry interest, such as health care, you may take elective courses focused on it. But beyond the few classes that are no-brainer selections, you must determine the ways that you will unlock knowledge from the right sources to propel you toward your career aspirations.

Consider the knowledge that you need to develop. Then think about the sources of that knowledge. It may be a certain course or a professor who is an expert in your area of interest, and it may also be your classmates or second-year students. For example, if you are pursuing investment management, in addition to introductory finance classes most business schools have advanced course work, such as derivatives and option pricing. Having a theoretical understanding of the material is not enough if you are going to successfully transition into the field. You may need to establish relationships with peers and professors who have worked in the field who can share the nuances of the industry or point you to additional resources to support your learning.

Business school is designed for individualized study. Of course, there will be required classes and activities that you complete in order to graduate, but much of your class time will be spent in elective courses that you select. You should choose electives based on the subject matter—taking classes that will round out the knowledge that you want to develop—and also on the projected impact of a given course. There are some classes that you should take with almost no regard for the subject. These classes are transformational, and you will refer back them throughout your career. I can't tell you which classes these are, as they are program-specific and likely also professor-specific. I had a few classes that I would put in this category. One was a leadership seminar on Thomas Jefferson, the founder of the University of Virginia. Over a seven-week period, we read the six volumes of Dumas Malone's *Jefferson and His Time* and discussed leadership while sitting in one of the original pavilions on the Lawn, the renowned site of so many pictures of the university. The conversations with Professor John Colley and my classmates really challenged me to consider my own definition of leadership and how I would respond when faced with difficult and unpopular choices.

Identify these transformational classes by talking with second-year students and alumni about their classroom experiences. Find out from them the classes that most impacted them, and determine the professors whose classes you must take. Business school professors are experienced professionals who serve as tour guides on your educational journey, and the best of them can make your classroom experience truly phenomenal.

Not all professors are created equal. Some are duds, leaving their students with little practical insight that they can apply in the future. But on the other end of the spectrum is what I call professor magic. Yes, magic. Basically all business school professors are incredibly intelligent, but not all of them are classroom magicians. Every top business school has some professors who fit this description. A great business school professor makes magic when she takes a topic and brings it to life for an entire classroom of students, not just a portion of the classroom. Remember that in business school, the backgrounds of a class of students can vary widely. Some have undergraduate business or quantitative undergraduate degrees and worked in business before school—these are the so-called quants—while others are so-called poets who have no background in business. Imagine teaching accounting to a class where 10 percent of the students are certified accountants and another 10 percent don't know the different between a debit and a credit. (Tip: If you don't know what debits and credits are, please take an accounting course prior to starting business school.)

The professor who can engage you whether you are a quant or a poet, challenge your thinking, and create experiences that will stick with you throughout your professional career is an amazing gift to you as a student. Make sure that you consider those elective courses taught by classroom magicians—you won't regret it!

Developing skills. The classroom experience is a very logical channel for increasing your knowledge; it is also a great place for developing your professional skills. Some courses are actually framed around skill building. In your first-year course work in particular, you will be pushed to develop your analytical and problem-solving skills in classes such as decision analysis, statistics, strategy, and ethics. There will also be classes that use different teaching formats that also enable you to practice your skills. For example, with case-based classes, in which a case study is used as the primary teaching tool, high student participation is required. This is a great opportunity for you to strengthen your communication skills.

Then there are classes that offer simulations—maybe you will participate in a mock negotiation where you have to defend your position against one of your classmate's positions, or perhaps you will be a mock trader in the stock market. These hands-on experiences allow you to practice in real-world conditions, develop your skills, and then see the results of your actions. Simulations are especially effective for career switchers—you will be able to gain experiences that you can apply in your new industry.

Finally there are immersions, which are the ultimate in applied learning. Many schools offer cultural and business immersions. With cultural immersions, or study abroad, you generally travel to another country and can build your cultural competence, practice another language, and experience business education in another part of the world. Business immersions, some of which are global, provide a consulting or internship-like experience. You may be part of a team that is advising a retailer on whether to enter a new market. Here you may apply your analytical, communication, and team-work skills—all with the guidance and support of your professors.

Initiating relationships. Your classroom experience will also be a strong channel for developing relationships in business school. Imagine being in your operations class, which meets three times per week for 75 minutes. You engage in a dialogue with 60 classmates and your professor for almost 4 hours every week for six to seven weeks. Although the conversations may be limited to one overarching topic of operations, you will learn a great deal about the backgrounds, knowledge, and experiences of your peers. You will also become familiar with some of the intangibles, such as how others engage (or don't) in the conversation, how they interact, and whether or not they respect their classmates. This is insight that you can use when selecting a study group or identifying a peer support group during the job search as well as in other professional relationships that you will need throughout your career.

Expect that you will need peer support to get through your course work. Investigate how study groups form on campus. The members of your study group may ultimately become some of your closest business school friends and contacts. When I was in business school, our study groups or learning teams were preassigned. We were expected to work with this group five nights a week for the entire first year. During our first week on campus, we participated in a required team-building exercise. You know the type—climb over a big wall and pull others up behind you. I have special bonds with the five people who were in my group, Learning Team 33—Team Superfly.

Finally, as you determine how you will initiate relationships, consider the optional classroom experiences, such as preterm activities. Many schools offer one- to two-week quantitative refreshers before the semester starts for incoming students who have been out of school for a long time or who don't have a quantitative background. This is a wonderful way to meet new people, as everyone is eager to find new friends.

INTEGRATING THE CLASSROOM EXPERIENCE WITH THE OTHER Cs

As you determine your approach to the classroom experience, you must consider it within the context of your club engagement, career exploration, and community and social life. These are not four distinctly separate channels but instead substantially overlap. For example, you may determine that you aspire to a leadership role in an industry-focused student club. While you may only be eligible for the position when you are a second-year student, with officer elections in the second semester of your first year, the classroom experience can help you lay the foundation for your leadership aspirations. The affinity that you build with the other students in your specific section, block, or cohort can serve as a base of support. At some schools you will be in classes with this same subset of your peers for the entire first year, while at other schools there will be different students in each of your classes. Your early classroom experiences may also offer your first foray into campus leadership. Many programs have elected representatives who provide leadership for the section or cohort. Immediately you can begin strengthening your brand and association with leadership on campus.

In the classroom, your peers will see your engagement as a student or as a student leader. This is a tremendous opportunity for you to showcase your personal brand, serving not only as the foundation for your club activities but also for your career exploration and developing a robust community and social life.

TO GUN OR NOT TO GUN?

As you can see, your time in the classroom will have a huge impact on your overall business school experience. It is a tremendous channel for building your knowledge, skills, and relationships in order to support your MBA slingshot. But I would be remiss if I didn't talk about your approach to the actual schoolwork.

In business school, there is often a strong culture of average or middling when it comes to performing in the classroom. With other graduate programs, such as law school and medical school, grades are used quite frequently as the basis for hiring decisions. Your business school grades won't likely carry that much weight. Your previous work experiences and skills will be used by recruiters as stronger indicators of your potential. Now, there are some industries that are more interested in grades overall or in specific courses. If you are pursuing an industry such as strategy consulting, you will be evaluated based on your GMAT scores as well as your grades. If you want to work in financial services, potential employers will likely want to know how you did in your finance classes.

Added to the middling phenomena in many top business schools are their nongrade disclosure policies, which discourage students from sharing their grades with employers until they have been hired. The theory is that if students don't have to share their grades, then they will take more risks in their course selection—not feeling as if they are limited to only those classes in which they can excel. We won't weigh the pros and cons of nongrade disclosure here, but generally speaking, in business school there is less focus on grades and academic honors than there is in other graduate programs.

What is exciting about business school and grades is that you get to decide where you want to aim. Of course, no one wants to be at the bottom of the class, barely passing the course. There are always jokes about the graduate with the highest grades having the same degree as the graduate with the lowest grades. But having worked in student affairs of a business school, I can tell you that the students who are at the bottom of the class do not have an experience that is comparable to their peers. Academic probation is real, as is academic dismissal. It is not common, but the fact that it happens at all should be enough to discourage any MBA student from aiming for the bottom. So, then, your options are top of the class or middle of the pack.

To gun or not to gun? That is the question. A gunner is a supercompetitive student who is aiming for the top of the class. Gunners are much more prevalent in law school and medical school than in business school, but they are present even in MBA programs. You have to decide if you are going to be a gunner or ride it out in the middle of the pack. Regardless of your approach to the classroom experience, your first priority should be to gain a strong foundation in business and management concepts in every class that you take. Whether you deem yourself a quant jock or not, commit to developing a robust understanding of finance, accounting, and statistics (or decision analysis). Resolve to *learn* these subjects, not just try to *get through* the classes. If you got into business school, then believe me, you are analytical enough to grasp the material regardless of your undergraduate major or pre–business school jobs.

If you choose the gunner route, obviously you want to earn good grades, but also consider setting your sights on your school's academic honors. At most business schools, top students are recognized at specific points during the program. It may be by semester, at the end of the first year, or at graduation. Talk with second-year students and professors to gain insight into how academic honors are awarded and to find out the criteria for the recognition.

If academic excellence is your aim and you want to be at the top of your class, then you will likely have your work cut out for you. It can be done, but you need to be aware of three realities of life. First, unlike undergraduate school, just about everyone in your class is capable of achieving high marks. Second, most business schools have a forced curve that allows only a small portion (5–10 percent) to get the top grade. And finally, testing well may not be enough to secure a high grade. Class participation, peer feedback, or professor input may also be considered in determining your final ranking.

Because academic honors are very difficult to achieve, many students don't aim for them. I wish more women would set their sights on academic honors and articulate that as a goal for themselves. You don't have to broadcast it to the world, but know that most people don't reach goals that they don't set. Too many of us undervalue our backgrounds and overrate other people who have more directly applicable experience.

You don't have to come from a quantitative background to achieve academic honors. A woman in my section did it. She worked hard. During class discussion she used her unique background to make insightful statements in class. She always moved the conversation forward, was eager to learn, and knew that she had much to share, even though it was different from what others brought to the classroom. She was a rock star.

If you want to be a gunner and you don't have an undergraduate degree in business, I strongly encourage you to take a few quantitative courses before you start school. The recommended courses may vary based on the school you attend, but you can't go wrong with statistics or finance. My third choice would be economics, followed by accounting. Instead of taking a class on accounting, pick up a book on accounting principles.

Now, let's consider the positives of being a gunner. You will build your brand of being a hard worker. Years after business school, I still remember my classmates who were serious students, and my prevailing impression of them now is that they are serious professionals whom I would highly recommend. As a gunner, you will probably learn more than your classmates. You will build stronger relationships with your professors, and you will position yourself for certain jobs.

There is downside to shooting for the top. Quite honestly, it requires lots of work, time, and energy, and it could require you to sacrifice other beneficial activities. Remember, you have to balance each of the 4 Cs. Further, that hyperfocus on being the best could have a negative impact on your brand. At some schools, it is not cool to look like a gunner. You may be perceived as uber-competitive or noncollegial.

So what about shooting for the middle of the pack? It is certainly a lot less work and stress. You can pick and choose the subjects and courses that you really want to dive into. You will also avoid the frustration of knowing that there are only a few slots at the top of the class. But alas, there is downside here too. Your brand could suffer. You may not be perceived as the smart, hardworking person that you are and might even be perceived as a slacker. You may not achieve all of the learning outcomes that you want, and there may be subjects in which your knowledge is not as robust as it should or could be. To avoid this, identify ways to really *learn* the material. I often find that students who are comfortable being in the middle shortcut some of their learning. For example, with their study groups, they use a simple divide-and-conquer strategy to get assignments, cases, and projects done. While this is efficient, it may hinder your ability to master the material.

JARGON ALERT

Best practices. The ideal. What managers identify as the best procedures in a company or field. Or what they say are the best.

Poet. An MBA student with no or limited quantitative background.

Quant jock. Someone who possesses exceptional skills in quantitative analysis, but sometimes this refers to students aspiring to careers in investment banking (though they may not have exceptional quantitative and analytical skills).

REVIEW: THE SHORT, SHORT VERSION

- The MBA classroom experience is intense and will overwhelm your initial weeks in business school, even if you have a strong quantitative background.
- Do your due diligence on your school's structure and learning mechanisms. Determine which ones will support your MBA slingshot in light of your ego, your aspirations, and your personal brand.
- Prepare for the academic rigor by taking a quantitative course or reading business-related books before you get to school. The more comfortable you feel with the concepts, the better able you will be to master them in the short time that you have.
- Understand the pros and cons of being a gunner and shooting for the top. In business school, you will be judged on more than grades.

Let's now look at the next business school channel: career exploration.

7

Career Exploration
Investigate or Concentrate?

The top priority of an MBA student is to get a post-MBA job. There are other goals, of course—to learn and become a better general manager, to build a powerful network, and to be positioned for long-term professional opportunities. But these and other aims seem pretty insignificant to MBA students who graduate without immediate and robust job prospects awaiting them. Attending business school is a long-term career investment, but all students want the short-term payout of a post-MBA job to set their career trajectory, enabling them to enter new industries or access higher-level positions.

With only about 21 months until graduation, you will be thrust into the job-search process upon arriving on campus. You will first journey through your internship search and then your full-time job search. While there are some established methods for navigating the search process during business school, MBA students secure internships and full-time jobs in many different ways. Some students land an internship offer months before even starting business school, while others don't finalize summer plans until weeks or even days before the end of the school year. Some students use the on-campus recruiting resources provided by the school's career services office, while others us their own contacts to find a position.

You will have to determine how you will effectively navigate your career exploration and job search while on campus. Many factors will impact your specific search process, but by and large the industry that you pursue and your school's connections to that industry are the most significant drivers.

Companies in industries that actively recruit MBA graduates in large numbers—investment banking, management consulting, and consumer packaged goods, for example—have prescribed steps that students take to be considered for opportunities. Generally speaking, if you are interested in one of these industries, you will have a well-defined blueprint to follow for the internship and the full-time job searches. For most other opportunities—with companies in industries that don't typically recruit MBA graduates or with smaller MBA hiring goals—the search process may be less defined and will require you to more proactively develop your own search strategy.

In reality, not all business schools are created equal, particularly when industry is considered. Even when companies in a particular industry covet MBA graduates, this doesn't mean that the companies will actively recruit students from your MBA program. Business schools have varying connections to industries based on their proximity to the industry hub and the number of alumni working in the industry and also through the school's efforts to cultivate industry relationships. For example, if you are considering technology, you can expect that the business schools near Silicon Valley have robust connections to that industry that you can leverage. They may also have a significant alumni base focused in the industry. A school in the southeastern United States may not have the same links, so a student then has to work a bit harder to transition into technology.

FINDING YOUR PATH

As you approach career exploration, your first task must be to understand the opportunities that you will have and the challenges that you will face as well as to identify all the resources that are available to you while in business school. Then you can determine how to leverage them to acquire the knowledge, skills, and relationships necessary to secure immediate professional opportunities—such as your summer internship and your first post-MBA job—and longer-term career opportunities and also to excel once you are in these roles. As you enter business school, at least one short-term objective should be clear—to use all available resources to get a full-time post-MBA job. This is an important objective—it might even be your most important one—but be mindful that it cannot be your only focus as you approach your career exploration in business school.

You want to do what is necessary to position yourself to get the full-time job that you want. But you want to make sure that you leave some time for career exploration activities that prepare you for jobs further along in your career and also allow you to explore options that you hadn't previously considered. This is all good in theory, but as a first-year MBA student with limited time and energy it can be difficult to excel at finding an internship, which is a very tactical undertaking, while also investigating various industry and fields, which can be quite nebulous and unstructured.

As a first-year student, should you concentrate your career-related activities on one goal of landing an internship, or should you investigate the various professional options that are available to you? Your answer to this question will shape your career-exploration approach when you get on campus.

Investigate different paths. If you are heading to business school, you should have already done research on different career paths and explored professional opportunities that might be of interest to you. Hopefully you have a good sense of your career aspirations. If you have absolutely no idea how you want to use your MBA professionally, then I strongly suggest that you explore that thoroughly *before* attending business school.

Even when you have articulated short-term and long-term goals, you may not be completely sure that you are on the right path for you. This is particularly true if your plans call for switching industries or fields. You are speculating that this is what you want to do professionally, but since you've never done it, you don't really know. Add to this uncertainty the overwhelming excitement that you will have when you learn more about what your classmates have done or plan to do after business school, and you may quickly begin to question your stated plans.

Generally, the students who are most successful in landing a position begin their internship search early. So does this mean that you should concentrate your search on one type of internship position immediately upon arriving on campus before you even explore other options? The truth is that your internship search will be much easier if you have laser-like focus on one path as soon as you arrive on campus. On the flip side, it will be exponentially more difficult if you don't know what you want to do. With that said, it is better to take the time to explore your options and figure out your goals while in business school than to wait until you are back in the workforce, perhaps in the wrong industry or career. Your MBA slingshot is designed to hit target aspirations, so you have to know where you want to go. If you have any doubt about your aspirations, then take time now to investigate what is out there.

As you investigate, know that you *will* feel pressured to pick a path— this means a specific industry, internship, and post-MBA job. Once you are on campus, expect that after "What is your name?" and "Where are you from?" the third question will be "What do you plan to do after business school?" Adding to the pressure to choose a path will be the anxiety of seeing peers who seem very clear about their pursuits. In fact, you may have deliberately come to business school to expand your career options, and while you have some idea of what you want to do, you may not be completely certain.

If any of this applies to you, then I encourage you to explore different paths. Don't have a wait-and-see attitude, hoping that your perfect career path will come to you in a dream. Instead, be very intentional about your career exploration to narrow your options. Attend relevant corporate presentations, conferences, and events that are held on campus to explore various industries and professions. Talk with your school's career services professionals, second-year students, and other first-year students to learn about their experiences and get suggestions. Treat these conversations like formal informational interviews. Prepare questions that you want to ask not just to learn more about their backgrounds but also to figure out how what they have done might connect to what you want to do.

While you may be unsure of your career path and are in the process of investigating your options, you don't want to appear wishy-washy—you want to present a strong personal brand that others can connect to. As people probe you about your professional interests, display what I call *thoughtful uncertainty.* Lead with your best guess of your ideal career path. Be direct, and don't hedge—just say it. Then you can mention one or two other areas that you may be considering. There is a pretty strong possibility that what you are leaning toward will end up being the path you take, especially in the short-term, so you should always get that out first. Then you can let people know the other alternatives that you are exploring.

As you take an investigative approach to career exploration, expect that you will connect with more people with different backgrounds, and you will hopefully uncover opportunities that you had never considered. You will give yourself the time and space to find the ideal career path. On the other hand, investigating takes more time and energy than concentrating on one path. You will likely attend more events, and you will have added stress in figuring out your path. The longer you delay the internship search, the harder it will be to get the one you want. It is not the end of the world if you don't land the perfect internship, but it can certainly make your full-time job search and transition to a new industry more difficult. In recent years, for example, many companies increasingly used summer interns as their primary source for full-time hires. This made it much harder for a second-year student who didn't intern at the company to secure a full-time job there.

As you explore, do so with some urgency. Set a date in your first semester by which you will solidify your internship search strategy to avoid missing out on time-sensitive opportunities and to minimize the disruption of taking an investigative approach to your career exploration. This should give you ample time to define your short-term goals and identify opportunities that may fit with what you think you want to do. With high-demand fields that have structured recruiting, such as financial services and consulting, it becomes more difficult, but not impossible, to access opportunities the longer you wait to pursue them. If industries such as these are on your list of possible paths, then start your industry prep work while still exploring your alternatives.

Most important, don't let the pressure to decide or to conform rob you of at least some time for exploration. Let me say it again. You will feel pressure to decide, as in right now. Don't give into it. Your internship and first post-MBA job are important, but in the scheme of your whole life, they are relatively minor.

Concentrate on one path. Hopefully, as you prepare for business school you are very clear about your short-term and long-term goals. You know where you want to go and can use business school to get you there. If that's the case, you can take a concentrated approach to career exploration, focusing your attention on one path. MBA programs were designed with you in mind. At some schools, recruiting activities begin within four weeks of starting classes. Surely students can't identify new career paths in that time, so business schools clearly expect that most students will come to campus with at least clear short-term goals. Business schools can then facilitate connections to alumni who can advise and support you and link you to companies that can hire you.

When you have a clear career focus, you are better able to plan and determine the steps you need to take in the internship search. You will be more readily able to identify the industry knowledge that you need to learn, the skills that you need to develop to make you more marketable, and the relationships that you should build in order to connect with people who can help you land your ideal internship. In addition to the clarity that comes from taking a concentrated approach to career exploration, you increase your chances of success. The internship search requires a lot of time and effort, even when you know what you want to do, so you want to get started as early as you can to achieve the best possible result.

The internship search is stressful but is a lot less so when you take a concentrated approach. When you can articulate what you want to do, you are better able to identify where you need help and link back to your personal brand, and others can more easily determine ways that they can be helpful to you.

While being able to take a concentrated approach is the ideal way to pursue career exploration in business school, there is some potential downside. When you have tunnel vision about your career path, you run the risk of missing opportunities to learn about new things and to connect with certain alumni, students, and faculty outside of your area of interest. Also, while you may be clear about your goals today, life and career happen, and things may change down the road. If you didn't take any time to explore what else might be out there for you, when things change in the future you may have no idea which way to turn.

Whether you investigate or concentrate, business school is the perfect time in your life to explore. Not only are you taking a break from your work life, but the people around you are invested in supporting you through this career transition. As Monisha Kapili, a graduate of Harvard Business School, shared with me, "Spend time in school reflecting on what you want out of life. I think there's a tendency to get caught up in [what everyone else] is doing or following the herd. Instead, using your two years [to get exposure] to people and to try different things, I think that you can come out with some really great clarity on what you want."

FINDING A JOB

In business school you have the theoretical exercise of finding your future career path. And then there is the very practical matter of getting a job. We focus so much on landing the internship between the first and second year because it often lays the foundation for your post-MBA full-time job search. As you consider the actual internship search, frame it around three stages to getting an MBA internship offer. You've had a job and gone through the process of getting one before, so there is no secret here. First, you have the networking and exposure stage, which generally runs from mid-September through January but varies a bit by school. Then there is the application stage, from about December through March. And finally you have the interview stage, which runs from January to April. Of course, you aren't done when you receive the offer. You have to negotiate and accept it and then prepare for the internship, which generally starts in late May or early June.

Take full advantage of career services offerings, even if you are conducting an independent search. At top business schools, there are robust recruiting efforts to support your internship search. Many of the career-related activities and events are held on campus, with companies traveling in to recruit students. Most events on campus are coordinated through your school's career services office. While the names may vary—career services, career management, career development—they function in very similar ways. The career services office facilitates the on-campus recruiting process, which tends to be very structured. If you are pursuing industries with a strong on-campus recruiting presence, such as investment banking, management consulting, consumer packaged goods, and manufacturing, leveraging on-campus resources may be sufficient to access opportunities. Industries such as technology, nonprofit, and private equity may require a more independent search in which you are reaching out to alumni to make connections.

Whether you use the on-campus recruiting process or conduct a more independent search, leverage every available resource that career services and your school have to offer. They may provide job-search coaching, assessment tools, and preparation for interviews and may offer guidance in navigating your internship search. Career services professionals can also make introductions to alumni working in the companies or industries that you are interested in. There are a lot more students than career services employees, but don't let that deter you. Remember, you are in business school to develop knowledge, skills, and relationships, and if the career services office can help you get those, then don't be shy about asking.

Use second-year students, alumni, and industry professionals to determine the knowledge, skills, and relationships that you will need. In addition to career services, second-year students are a phenomenal resource. Second-year students just went through the internship recruiting process and can help you formulate the most appropriate career search strategy. They can help you identify faculty and alumni in your areas of interest or club and company events that may be useful. Second-year students can give you a sense of the time and work required for successful recruiting. As you gather information, don't just talk with the second-year students who were successful in securing their top jobs; also talk to those students who came up short in the process. This will help you determine what you need to do to best position yourself for success.

With access to current students, alumni, professors, and industry professionals, you will have many resources available to support you. Leverage them whether you are going through an on-campus or independent internship search. Particularly with students and alumni, they take great pride in helping first-year students. They got help when they were first-year students from graduates who came before them and want to pay it forward. They also want to make sure that you don't devalue the brand of the school by being unprepared.

Leverage on-campus recruiting for your independent search. With an independent search, you may have to find your own sources for internships, but you have access to significant resources. Don't ignore the traditional campus recruiting events, which can still provide valuable exposure and networking. With the exception of possibly alumni class reunions, more alumni and professionals visit campus in connection with on-campus recruiting than anything else. So, this may be your best chance to network with alumni and professionals in related fields, even if you aren't interested in their particular industry or company. For example, if you are interested in health care consulting firms, which don't recruit on your campus, you still may find corporate events hosted by health care and insurance companies or management consulting firms helpful in developing your knowledge about the industry.

Carefully manage your time. Many companies host two- to three-hour sessions on campus to educate students on the industry, the company, and roles within the organization. The companies want to market themselves and their opportunities to students. During the peak presentation season, there may be four to six corporate presentations per day held in the afternoons and evenings four days per week at your school. Of course, the companies span a number of industries, but it is not hard to imagine that internship search activities could quickly fill up your calendar.

In addition to general presentations, many companies will host more intimate events for select groups of students. Many companies have targeted efforts to recruit women, so you may be invited to additional small receptions, dinners, and other events. It can be very difficult to decline events, particularly with companies where you are interested in working. On the other hand, you can't be everywhere at once, and you have other obligations and interests outside of finding a job. Don't feel like you to have to say "yes" to every invitation. If you do decline, send a thoughtful note to reiterate your interest.

Rethink what preparation means. I am a former MBA recruiter. Having interviewed students at top MBA programs across the country, I can tell you that many candidates were not prepared. I was hiring for financial services roles, so the interview was challenging, but in many cases candidates couldn't get through the basic finance questions. That's bad!

When you interview for internships, you may be asked technical questions or challenging open-ended questions, such as explaining the current state of the economy, or you may be asked problem-solving questions, such as "How many sheep are there in Switzerland?" Being successful in interviews is all about preparation. Technically women *are* preparing for interviews, but all too often we aren't preparing in the right ways to get the offer. We practice answering questions, figuring out the answers we would give if asked. But we may not fully understand the underlying principles of what we are trying to articulate. This is particularly true with candidates who are seeking opportunities in a new field. If that is your situation, even a slightly different question can derail you from the response you have memorized. Dig deeper. And yes, ask for help.

Let's assume for a moment that you are a career switcher. You have been successful in one field, and now you are getting an MBA and are looking at a different field entirely. When you interview with a company, you are essentially saying, "I know almost nothing about this industry, and I want you to pay me six figures to train me." That's fine. But I, the recruiter, want you to show me that you have what it takes. You need to go all out to demonstrate that you are worth the investment. Put ego aside, and do whatever it takes. Regardless of whether it is raising your hand in the classroom so you can get comfortable talking about a certain topic, spending time with the professor, or reading the *Wall Street Journal* or *Ad Age* constantly, just do what you need to do, because if you don't, you won't get what you want.

Finally, being well prepared for interviews requires pushing aside your fear of rejection. Men have been rejected a lot more (thanks to us), and they roll with it better. Women, often very successful women, have a hard time being wrong. We work really hard and put in extra hours so that when we share our position, we are correct. We may get more flustered when we aren't sure of an answer. In our daily lives, we manage this by fully researching things in advance so that we are ready for any questions that may come up. But many interviews, particularly at the MBA level, are designed so that you can't prepare your answer in advance. Instead, you will have to process it with your interviewer during the interview, so you might be wrong. While you can't prepare an answer, you can prepare yourself. Get help from others, and find opportunities where you can take risks—commenting on things that you may be less confident talking about. You can't do it alone, and there are people who can help you. Talk to them.

JARGON ALERT

Eat what you kill. Often used in sales- and commission-based environments to denote that you get paid based on your own initiative and effort.

Monetize. A verb made popular in the Internet industry to find new ways to make money from a product or service.

Net-net. An investing technique, though you will likely hear it misused as a superfluous phrase for the end result or the bottom line.

REVIEW: THE SHORT, SHORT VERSION

- Once you have defined your aspirations, determine your career search strategy (on-campus, independent search, or a combination) and what that means for your first semester on campus.

- Some industries can only be pursued off campus. You will need to be a self-starter.
- If you aren't sure what you want to do, take your time, but know that the career clock is ticking.
- Leverage your school's career services office and other resources.
- To excel in interviews, get over your fear of rejection.

Next we'll look at an area where women often don't give enough thought to in planning: club activities.

8

More Than Résumé Bullets
Leveraging Club Activities

Club: noun. An association of persons, for some common objective, usually jointly supported and meeting periodically.

Club: verb. To beat or strike with, or as if with, a club.

There is a big difference between joining a club and being clubbed by too many commitments. While you may be thinking now that you won't over-commit yourself, if you are like most women, when you get on campus you will take on too many club and cocurricular activities. When you find that your first-year cohort is amazing, of course, you will be honored to take on a cohort leadership role. Wine? You like wine. So the wine club seems like the perfect way to meet people who also like wine. Oh, and you just heard that they are looking for students to plan an international immersion trip to Bahrain over spring break. That sounds incredible. Soon you find that you are getting clubbed, from an unintentional lapse that occurred when you were invigorated by all that was new and exciting around you.

At this point in the book, we are halfway through outlining the four channels that you will use to develop the knowledge, skills, and relationships of your MBA slingshot: classroom experience and career exploration, which we have already discussed; club engagement, which we will cover in this chapter; and community and social life, which we will get to in the next chapter. Of all plans that you will make and the options that you will select as you approach the 4 Cs, limiting your club engagement will likely be the hardest to adhere to. So many more activities will call to you than you have the time or energy to complete. While you may ultimately extend your-self a bit more than you originally had planned, make sure that whatever you undertake strengthens your MBA slingshot and doesn't weaken it.

STUDENT CLUBS

Club engagement is an important aspect of your MBA slingshot, as it provides you with the most balanced access to knowledge, skills, and relationships while you are in school. To develop your expertise in interna-tional business, you might attend an emerging markets conference hosted by the Latin American student association. Or you might take part in a marketing simulation that is organized by the marketing club in partner-ship with a consumer packaged goods company. Or you could join the student government organization to facilitate access to your school's administration. You will have so many choices when it comes to your student club participation.

In business school, the majority of activities and events will be coordi-nated by or in conjunction with student clubs and organizations, so it is no surprise that clubs often drive the school environment. Clubs will serve as important mechanisms for you to use in engaging with the community and building relationships. They will enable you to meet people beyond those in your classes, particularly with second-year students and classmates with similar interests. When MBA alumni share stories about business school, their club involvement often comes up. In my research, this is one of the areas where women wish they had developed a strategy before school—not just to avoid overcommitting themselves but also to consider which clubs would enable them to meet a broader range of their classmates and also to better position themselves for leadership positions on campus.

With student clubs, each has a focus. They may be related to career, civic/volunteer, student government, or social/special interests. You will benefit from involvement with different types of clubs, though you shouldn't try to tackle all of them.

Career-focused clubs are generally the most popular—just about every MBA student is in at least one career-focused club. These allow you to con-nect with people who have similar professional interests and to develop skills and knowledge that you can leverage in your career. In addition, many companies build relationships with career-focused club leaders to share job opportunities and to engage in the club's activities, such as conferences and panel discussions.

Civic/volunteer clubs give you an opportunity to impact the local, na-tional, and global communities through traditional and unique community service activities. The school and student government clubs enable you to impact how the school is run. You might serve as a class officer, on the student admissions committee, or as an orientation leader for incoming first-year students. Then there are the special interest clubs, which are largely social in nature. These clubs allow you to learn something new and connect with people who have similar interests. You may have a hobby, such as singing or writing, that you can cultivate through a campus a cappella group or the student newspaper. Or you might join the business school's intermural flag football team or visit different wineries with the wine club to learn more about the wine industry and the art of wine tasting.

While some clubs have a very specific focus, many serve various purposes. When you have limited time to commit to multiple clubs, these hybrid clubs are a great option, as they consolidate many functions within one club. For example, I was very active in the Graduate Women in Business (GWIB) student organization. GWIB, like many affinity-based clubs, is partly career-focused but also provides support and raises awareness about the culture or group. That variety was very appealing to me. Through GWIB I received career support, but I also volunteered and raised money for a local women's shelter. For two years, I served as one of the two auctioneers at the annual auction, which in addition to being a huge honor gave me great visibility in the community. Through the auction I also gained experience in planning major events, which has been an important skill in my career.

APPROACH TO CLUB ENGAGEMENT

It would be great to do it all, but there are limits. As you plan for business school, consider how you will approach your club engagement. There will be some clubs that you definitely want to join, such as the ones linked to your professional interests. Before you commit to other clubs, determine what you hope to gain from your club involvement. Do you want to develop skills, knowledge, and/or relationships? Do you want to strengthen your résumé or access opportunities that come with membership? Do you want to impact and help others?

You may be able to decide your approach to club engagement before you arrive on campus, but more than likely you will still have some open questions when you start school. To prepare yourself, make a list of the clubs that you would consider joining. Then when you arrive on campus, you can investigate them more to decide whether to join. Beyond your interests, there are several considerations as you select clubs.

Leadership aspirations. You may be keen on taking on a club leadership role. At most schools, leadership positions are awarded in the spring of your first year, although some may be available in your first semester. So, there isn't much time to get acclimated. Even if you are not sure that you want a leadership position at this point, you still want to establish yourself in the club as someone with leadership potential.

Capacity. When you join a club, you should commit to being an active participant—building relationships, attending events, and in some cases helping with the administration of club activities. You receive all of the club's benefits in return for your commitment. But make sure that you understand your responsibilities and determine whether you have the capacity as well as the time and energy required. At the Johnson Graduate School of Management at Cornell University, one of the largest clubs is Community Impact. In addition to volunteer activities, students can be community consultants, working on pro bono consulting projects in the local community. This is a tremendous way to put new skills and knowledge into action, but it is not an exercise. You have a real client with a real issue, so you can't just decide not to show up because you are overcommitted.

Club quality. Just because a club is listed on your school's website and may have a few members doesn't mean that it is vibrant and conducive to your goals. Unless you have a strong desire to revive a student club, position yourself with groups that are already strong.

Participant only. There may be clubs in which you have an interest but don't need to be a full member of to take advantage of the benefits. It is akin to an associate membership. You can take advantage of the most appealing club events without any additional obligations. Also investigate the many club-sponsored activities that are open to all students and are not limited to members only.

Depth versus breadth. While overcommitting to clubs should definitely not be your approach to club engagement, you will have to decide whether to get deeply involved with one or two clubs or to participate more broadly.

Charisse Conanan, a University of Chicago Booth School of Business grad and the founder of Smarteys, suggested that "because business school can be very distracting, . . . pick two or three things that you want to do in business school and do those well. Forget everything else. Whatever it is, you're going to have to make a trade-off." If you choose to engage deeply with one or two clubs, you will probably be able to build deeper relationships and gain more knowledge. You won't be spreading your time over several clubs; you will be able to prioritize the one or two that you do join and be better positioned to take a leadership position in the future. You may also position yourself to have greater impact because you are really able to commit yourself fully to the projects that you undertake. When you participate in one or two clubs, you can more easily present a cohesive personal brand, showcasing to others what is important to you. On the downside, when you focus on only one or two clubs, you may reduce your ability to engage with a variety of activities and with different people. You want to be careful not to bury yourself in one area—you have to come up for air.

If you decide that you want more variety with your club choices, you will likely get broader exposure to many different things that are offered at your school. Also, your club engagement has the potential to meet more of your needs, from career to social to civic. And you will have the full experience, akin to what so many MBA students had before you, however draining. In addition to club involvement being both exhausting and overwhelming, you will likely have lots of time conflicts. Ultimately you will have to choose which clubs to prioritize.

CAREER-FOCUSED CLUB ENGAGEMENT

Your approach to club engagement is yours to create. My strong suggestion to you, though, is that you prioritize one career-focused club that will position you for your short-term goals. Research the clubs on your campus and determine the career-focused clubs that most closely align with your professional aspirations. If you want to work in marketing and there is marketing club, take advantage of the opportunity. At Chicago Booth there are more than 70 student groups, with more than 20 that are career-focused. If you are interested in working in a senior role in the health care industry, there are two clubs that might interest you—the Healthcare Group and the Corporate Management & Strategy Group. Consider joining both. Doing so will give you access to the group listserv, members, and events. Once you do that, prioritize only one. If you have a choice of career-focused clubs, consider the strength of the club's infrastructure, reputation, and faculty adviser.

As a member, build strong relationships with career club leaders, particularly when you are involved with a club that aligns with your short-term goals. Depending on the school and the club, leaders and faculty advisers may have some influence in the recruiting process, as they interact with corporate representatives on behalf of the club. Companies may ask club leaders for recommendations on first-year students to target for internship opportunities. I wouldn't focus on this, but it is good to know that club leadership has its privileges.

Club engagement must be part of your business school experience. As you decide where you will plug in, begin with what will help you strengthen your MBA slingshot.

JARGON ALERT

Out of pocket. Not around. Unavailable.

Peel back the onion. A phrase meaning to dig deeper to find an answer or a layer-by-layer analysis.

Quick win. Rapid, easy, and lucrative results.

REVIEW: THE SHORT, SHORT VERSION

- Club engagement is an important aspect of your MBA slingshot, as it provides you with the most balanced access to knowledge, skills, and relationships while you are in school.
- Many women overcommit to clubs. Don't give in to the temptation. Focus.
- There are student clubs related to career, civic/volunteer, student government, and social/special interests.
- In selecting clubs, consider your interests, leadership aspirations, capacity, and the club quality and benefits.
- Prioritize one career-focused club that will position you for your short-term goals.

You are making some tough decisions, and now you need to make even more. How will you approach community and social life?

9

B-School Life
Building a Sense of Community

"Eat, drink and be merry!" From a Bible verse, of all places, that phrase truly encompasses how people connect in profound and meaningful ways in MBA programs. Whether through breaking bread, throwing back a few drinks, or laughing together, business school fosters bonds that extend beyond anything words could convey. Think about any culture or community. Food, alcohol, and/or laughter are critical to the way connections between people are formed. Business school is no different, which is why your social life and interactions are so important to your MBA experience and community engagement.

When you make the decision to attend a particular business school, you also make the corresponding decision to join that school's community. Upon stepping on the campus, you will become part of an all-encompassing MBA community. You will see and interact with your peers, professors, and others seemingly nonstop for two years on and off campus. What makes the full-time MBA program so different from undergrad and work settings is the significant overlap of classroom, career, and club activities with your social life. It is often difficult to distinguish between what is personal and professional, between what is on the record and off the record.

The fourth C of the 4 Cs is community and social life. Technically, your classroom experience, career exploration, and club engagement are part of your community experience, but I want to separate out the social activities that make up the MBA experience. Community and social activities range from the casual happy hour after class on Thursday to an international food festival in which your classmates from different cultures share their cuisines and customs to annual parties that celebrate often random school traditions. These social interactions will significantly impact your time at business school and the relationships that you build.

Your approach to community engagement has two main elements: the events and activities you attend and the people with whom you interact.

BUSINESS SCHOOL EVENTS AND ACTIVITIES

In your first weeks and months on campus, you will lay the foundation for community engagement with the events and activities in which you participate. Frankly, this starts before school with admissions events the previous fall, admitted students' weekend in the spring, and connecting through networking events and online forums during the summer before school starts. These interactions will begin to form your community engagement approach. All of these preterm events are very useful, but they are also optional. You have to determine what you will participate in. While I would recommend getting engaged early, you may opt instead to wait until business school starts in the fall. There is no right answer, only the right answer for you.

Once school starts, you will find that the breadth of community and social events in which you can engage is quite broad. You might attend informal dinners and happy hours with a few folks who live in your building or with your friend who met someone else in the bookstore who had two other friends who were going to dinner. Then there are the coordinated events, possibly with your section or cohort, your entire first-year MBA class, or the entire community, such as school-wide social and cultural events. The opportunities for engagement don't end there. While likely not your first priority, don't forget that your business school is part of a larger university and a local community that you can include in your engagement plan. For example, when I was in grad school I acted in two plays at local Charlottesville community theaters, allowing me to connect in a distinctly unique way outside of my business school experience.

Community engagement will also extend beyond the campus footprint. You might travel with your classmates to a case competition, to a softball tournament hosted by another MBA program, or to Winter Carnival at the Tuck School of Business at Dartmouth. Competing against other schools really heightens bonding among your peers and enables you to broaden your relationship building to other MBA programs.

Trying new things. There are truly limitless opportunities for building community while in business school. Choosing how to deal with the many social activities and options can feel like gambling—and we all have different betting strategies. Some people put all their chips in and just go for it. They are not going to take their time and find out if the table is hot. Instead, they are going to put it all in and hope to win. When it comes to community and social life, there is little planning with this type of MBA student—these people simply go for it and take the if-there's-a-party-I-am-there approach. Other people show more restraint in their betting. They pick and choose when to play. In some cases, though, three games later they may still be standing off to the side and contemplating whether to join in, while winners are walking away from the table with the prize.

Don't be afraid to try new things and participate in a range of activities. Diversity is the spice of life, right? As you determine how you will engage in the community, try not to be limited by what you do or don't like based on past experiences. Instead, consider participating in activities that enable you to connect with your classmates and community in different ways. Let's use sports as an example. I love sports and I love football (Go Giants!), but not everyone is a sports fan. Many people would say that this tends to be gender-based—that women are less likely to enjoy watching sports. I actually just think that women, compared to men, are more comfortable with and less stigmatized for saying that they don't like sports. I suggest that when you get to business school if you have never been to a football tailgate because you don't particularly like sports, try it out—especially if you attend a school with a huge football tradition.

Pregame tailgating might be a way to stretch yourself without having to be inauthentic, because the event has nothing to do with the actual football game. In fact, you don't even have to go to the game. You could just go to the pregame festivities. Certainly your life won't be over if you skip every sporting event, but you might consider attending for the tradition of the community coming together and rallying as a group. Particularly if you attend a business school that is part of a university with a long football tradition, such as the University of Michigan, Ohio State University, or the University of Southern California, expect that for the rest of your life when you mention your alma mater, you will be asked about football. And you will have a cool memory of keg stands in the parking lot. I'm kidding. No keg stands! They are wrong on so many levels!

Traditions and must-do activities. Figure out your school's traditions, and identify the must-do activities. If you are a first-year student at Duke University's Fuqua School of Business, Campout deserves consideration as a must-do event. Two thousand graduate and undergraduate students sharing 36 wild hours of camping out to get season passes for men's basketball. Seven hundred fifty passes are available, and surviving Campout takes resilience. The basketball committee rings a siren at all hours, and you check in at a central tent. If you make it through all of the check-ins, you are entered into a lottery for the tickets. In the meantime, you might participate in a free-throw competition, a football game–watching party, or speed dating. It's crazy, but it is a tradition, part of the experience of attending Duke.

Stanford Graduate School of Business students hold weekly Friends of Arjay Miller (FOAM) parties. Named after a former dean, these FOAM parties, as they are called, culminate in an annual Las Vegas FOAM party night, complete with 1970s costumes. I was visiting campus on the day the students were heading to Vegas. Their costumes were ridiculous (and totally awesome). Students party all night and then fly back for class, bonding and bragging about how much sleep they missed.

Darden has the 100-case party to celebrate getting through—you guessed it—the first 100 case discussions. We also have the Foxfield Horse Races. Now, I think that it is totally random for people to get dressed up and go watch horses run around in circles, but I was out there with all of my classmates. Foxfield, a steeplechase race that originated in 1978, is a community and University of Virginia tradition. Attendees dress up as Southern aristocrats with bow ties, seersucker suits, and floppy hats and drink bourbon, lots of it. Because it is a tailgating event there is no grandstand, so you can't actually see much of the race or see who wins. But that's not the point. Will I ever return to that event? Probably not. Yet it was the kind of experience that connected me to that university. I'm excited that I can say, "I did that."

You don't have to do everything. Even with activities that are school traditions and are very popular with MBA students, you may decide that they are not must-do activities for you.

FOMO syndrome. Ultimately, the biggest challenge in business school is not course work but managing your schedule to fit everything in—the fun, the bonding, the relationship-building opportunities, career activities, and club responsibilities. Plus, there are the textbooks, articles, and cases to read; problem sets to complete; and sleep to catch up on. There will be trade-offs, and you need to decide what is most important to you.

As you get involved on campus, whether with social events or educational and club activities, you are sure to come face-to-face with the dreaded FOMO syndrome. That's *fear of missing out.* With FOMO, you are scared to miss any event for fear that the one you choose to skip will be the one that everyone deems as the greatest of the year, whether it is a dynamic speaker who was only on campus for one day or the ultimate party. So, to avoid FOMO you try to go to everything.

FOMO can make you so busy and unfocused that you don't enjoy any of the social events you are so intent on taking part in. It is really taxing mentally and physically to try to do everything. And oh, by the way, you can't do everything—you will have overlaps and conflicts to contend with. Your best bet is to make deliberate choices about your activities and accept that you will miss out on some fun stuff. This is a certainty. Just make sure that the events you skip aren't ones that you will regret missing because FOMO had you doing something else that you really didn't care about.

ENGAGING WITH OTHERS

As you engage in the MBA experience, your personal community will immediately take shape around you. Small boot-camp style environments such as business school breed fast friendships. With time, many of these initial relationships will become real and lasting friendships. At first, though, they will be pseudofriendships, which is not inherently a bad thing. From those initial friendships, your business school clique, though likely unintentional, will begin to form. Even with the best intentions of developing a diverse circle of friends, you may find yourself in a relatively homogenous group.

As you manage your community and social life, be mindful of the people with whom you align yourself. You don't have to run background checks and interview each person to determine if she or he can be in your circle of friends, but instead you want to consider how you use the community component to build the knowledge, skills, and particularly the relationships that will help you position your MBA slingshot.

Any community is all about the people in it. You will begin to interact with the members of your MBA community long before you step on campus, whether at school-sponsored admissions events or possibly during admitted students' weekend. And you will make decisions that can greatly impact how you interact with others in the community. Particularly when you are moving to a new city, as many MBA students do, you need an apartment and possibly a roommate. As you downsize to a student budget, you may seek a roommate to reduce your housing costs. Your roommate decision should extend beyond the I-will-get-a-roommate-because-it-is-cheaper approach, because your decision can impact your community engagement, particularly when you live with a fellow MBA student. When you attend those first events on campus, that roommate will likely be the person you are walking in with, a person others may associate with you.

With your roommate you may attend events together, and you both can quickly become part of the same circle of friends. If a strained or bad relationship forms, this can also affect how you interact with your roommate and even your roommate's friends. Most of us don't conduct a thorough roommate screening. I mean, it is only a year, and particularly when you have your own bedroom and bathroom, it doesn't seem like that big of a deal. You might not be that finicky about your personal space, but regardless of your comfort level, be thoughtful in your roommate selection.

You might choose to live with someone who is from a different background or experience for a bit of a cultural exchange, or you might determine that you want a roommate who is similar to you because you want your apartment to feel much like your previous living spaces, like home. Also consider your roommate's personality and how this could impact your social life and engagement in the MBA community. If you tend to be introverted and aren't normally very social, what type of roommate will suit you best? You may determine that during your first year of business school, you want to be very socially engaged in order to challenge yourself and strengthen your relationship management skills. Having an outgoing, active roommate could be a great first step. On the other hand, this type of roommate might be overwhelming to you. Give some thought to what you want before you sign the lease on the dotted line, and talk to each other about the roommate relationship, what you expect, and what you have to offer.

The other housing decision that can greatly impact your community engagement is where you decide to live, specifically your proximity to campus and to other MBA students. If you live far from campus, you may leave early for class and not get back home until late at night. When it is not convenient to go home in the middle of the day, you may find that you spend more time on campus. The downside of this is that when you do go home, you may be less likely to make the trek back out to school and community activities. Living close to school can make participation in activities a bit more feasible and likely.

At many business schools, there are apartment complexes close to campus that are both popular and filled with MBA students. At Darden, it is Ivy Gardens. At Northwestern's Kellogg School of Management, it is Evanston Place or Park Evanston, and at Stanford Graduate School of Business, it is the Schwab Residential Center. When you live in one of these communities, you are basically surrounded by your classmates at all times. While you will technically have the privacy of your own apartment, your neighbors will see you coming and going. And they will also see people coming and going from your place. You may party with or possibly even date your neighbors—that may be too close for comfort.

Incoming MBA students want to quickly check the tasks of "find a place to live" and "find a roommate" off their to-do lists. But these decisions can have a significant impact on your community and social life. Give thought to the living environment that will be most successful in light of the knowledge, skills, and relationships that you want to build and experience that you want to have while in business school.

SHARE AFFINITY

Part of the reason that so many professionals choose to get their MBA degrees is because they want to build relationships with people from diverse backgrounds and experiences. While I find that MBA students today—the majority of whom are from the millennial generation born after 1982 and began college in the new millennium—are more open to working with people from different backgrounds, business school communities aren't quite the melting pot that we might expect.

I want to offer you a challenge as you develop your approach to community and social life. As you engage with others in business school, share affinity and not just space with other students, faculty, and staff. Let me explain. At so many business schools and frankly just about everywhere, people self-segregate into subgroups, and they have limited interactions with other subgroups. The subgroups may form around gender, ethnicity, nationality, or interests. In business school, they may form around section, professional aspirations, background, or living situations.

We naturally form affinity groups and affiliations as humans. This allows us to quickly find people we relate to, which can lead to even deeper bonds. This innate need to associate with those who are similar can make it more difficult to connect with other people who are different from us and leads to a community of subgroups colocated in the same space. In U.S. professional environments, gender and ethnicity often come up as dominant subgroup differentiators. In the business school environment, I would add country of origin, native language, and professional background and interests as stark dividers within the community.

Let me give you an example. Imagine that in your first-year cohort you are American and sit next to a classmate who is from China. Each morning before class starts, the two of you chat for two or three minutes, and he tells you funny stories about acclimating to life in the United States. When you see him outside of class, you always say hi, but you don't actually interact beyond that. He is usually with other Asian students; in fact, sometimes they aren't speaking English. You stick with your friends, and he sticks with his. Upon graduation you have fond memories of your Chinese classmate, but when you think about it, you realize that you never learned much about him personally.

This is classic colocating community behavior in which we feel like we know people because we see them every day and we exchange pleasantries, but we actually know nothing substantive about them and vice versa. This is particularly prevalent among domestic and international MBA students in business school, possibly because of cultural and language barriers, but the subgroups could be aspiring investment bankers versus aspiring brand managers or partiers versus those who don't drink. Subgroups always emerge, and the associations can become deeply entrenched.

I am not suggesting that every conversation needs to be a cultural exchange; sometimes you want to be with people with similar backgrounds in order to unwind or have mindless conversation. But too often we stick with who and what we know and miss opportunities to build richer community. As you engage in business school, make the determination to share not just space but affinity and interest with other members of the community. Be curious about people, get to know them, and take an interest in their differences and commonalities. Build relationships with people you wouldn't normally be drawn to. You don't have to be BFFs, but you can be true community members. Do this by inviting others into your subgroup. If your friends are going to happy hour, invite someone new. Occasionally insert yourself into others' subgroups by joining a conversation or attending an event that, while not generally your preference, might be common for another subgroup.

Connecting across subgroups gets you out of your comfort zone, which is a good thing. It helps you develop cultural competence and learn new things while you enhance someone else's experience. Besides, you will have friends in cool places whom you can visit for years to come.

FINAL COMMUNITY ENGAGEMENT THOUGHT: MUCH BOOZING ADVISED?

Business school is social, and there is lots of drinking (except maybe at the Marriott School of Management at Brigham Young University). *The Economist* says that the MBA should stand for "Much Boozing Advised." There is generally alcohol at every school- or corporate-sponsored event. Oh yeah, and then you have the actual social events, such as happy hours and parties—not just at the rowdy parties, either. Expect that people will be drinking at the charity fund-raiser or the family-friendly food festival. You might have a glass of wine in your hand as you talk with a classmate with her two-year-old child darting back and forth across the room.

While MBA social events are generally respectful and responsible, there may be a party or two that resembles *Animal House*. As a woman, prioritize your personal safety (and your self-respect, if that's important to you). You need to know what your limits are. If you can only have two glasses of wine and keep your wits about you, don't drink the third glass— even if this means that you have to casually find a place to dump the drink. (Although tossing the drink might technically be deemed alcohol abuse, it is for a good reason! Just kidding!) While alcoholic beverages will be served at almost every business school function, don't feel that you have to drink excessively to fit in, and don't let that stop you from actively participating.

Also, know who your friends are. Not to be totally dramatic here, but unless you happen to attend business school with one of your closest friends, assume that you have no friends there. Expect that you will have to take care of yourself. School is so much fun, and from the hundreds and hundreds of MBA students I have known and worked with over the years, I've heard of only a handful of incidents where students felt unsafe or in awkward compromising positions. But it does happen. This brings me to a quick note on personal brand.

Because there is a blurry line between your personal and professional brand in business school, make sure you won't be mortified on Monday morning when people are relaying what you did at a party on Friday night. I want you to be mindful of lurking smartphones, Instagram, and Facebook, yet don't be so fearful of making a mistake or of damaging your brand that you can't relax and be yourself. Social life and community engagement, at their core, are about having fun and connecting with people. It's all right to let your hair down a little bit.

Determine the must-do activities and events as early as possible. Get expert advice from second-year students. They were in your shoes a year ago. Remember that you don't have to do everything, but find those events and activities that are unique to your business school and that connect you to your classmates, faculty, and past and future alumni. Then mark your calendar!

JARGON ALERT

Economies of scale. Cost advantage and efficiency gained from generating more of a product. Often used as a rationale for growth.

Soup to nuts. To create every aspect of something from beginning to end.

Wet signature. Using an actual human signature instead of an electronic one on important things, such as contracts.

REVIEW: THE SHORT, SHORT VERSION

- Try new things, and participate in a range of activities.
- Take part in the traditions of your school, even the crazy ones.
- Know that you will miss out on some things, so choose carefully.
- If you don't decide the kind of community and social life that you want, you will be a victim of chance. Seriously consider how you want to live, where you want to live, and with whom.
- Don't just share space; share affinity with members of the business school community.

Now that we've covered the 4 Cs, let's turn our attention toward the MBA assets, starting with knowledge.

10

So You Say You Are an MBA?
Developing the Knowledge and
Expertise to Lead

When graduation day finally arrives 21 months after you begin business school, you will be able to call yourself an MBA. At that point you can expect to have higher earning potential and access to greater professional opportunities. These benefits are not bestowed upon you because of your designation as an MBA but instead are a result of your ability to proficiently deploy your MBA assets—knowledge, skills, and relationships—in your career. Let's explore each of these MBA assets separately over the next three chapters, starting here with MBA knowledge.

GENERAL MANAGEMENT

The MBA is a general management degree. While many business school alumni will say that they got an MBA in a specific area, such as marketing or finance, that's not quite true. Instead, the MBA prepared them to be a management generalist. And then through a major or concentration that their schools offered, those alumni developed greater expertise in a particular subject area. The MBA degree by definition is broad in scope. So, if you really want a degree in finance, wanting only to learn about finance, then you would be better served pursuing a master's of science in finance instead of an MBA.

In your journey to develop a strong general management foundation during business school, you will be required to take core courses in several different subjects, including marketing, finance, accounting, statistics, leadership/organizational behavior, ethics, economics, strategy, and operations. You will learn these subjects in a roomful of MBA students whose level of subject-matter expertise will vary widely. Your mastery of operations if you are pursuing nonprofit opportunities might be substantially different than your peer who is pursuing a career in supply-chain management. You and your classmates will use your education in diverse functions and industries after graduation. But bringing you together in one business school classroom enables you each to see the varied applications of critical management concepts and develop a more comprehensive management perspective to make adept decisions in your own field.

Whether or not operations management is your intended career path, you must have some level of proficiency in the subject if you are to credibly call yourself an MBA. The same is true of all of your core MBA courses. You don't have to be an expert on every subject, but a robust foundation of knowledge and understanding of how the various subjects relate to one another is required. Consider expertise in any given subject on a knowledge continuum that ranges from novice at the lowest level to advance beginner and then to competent and then, at the highest level, to expert. When you are first introduced to a concept, you are a novice. For my poets with no business background, your first task will be to acquire information and get the basics to reach novice status. Hopefully, you can accomplish this before business school begins.

After novice, the next stages in the knowledge continuum are advanced beginner and then competent. Particularly for those new to general management education, advanced beginner is the minimum acceptable standard for any core business subject if you want to call yourself an MBA. An advanced beginner in first-year finance might be able to get her financial models to work properly, being able to show a solid understanding of the basics. At the end of your first semester of business school, you would then know enough to get a passing grade in your finance course but would still have critical gaps in your subject-matter knowledge. Reaching true competence in finance may require more advanced coursework, enabling you to master the underlying financial concepts with the ability to apply them broadly. Your MBA program may not require that you take any more finance courses beyond the first-year course to graduate, so you will have to actively choose to continue to advance on the finance knowledge continuum. It is up to you to decide your education plan, but remember that you are in business school to lay the foundation to become a competent general manager, not an advanced beginner general manager.

You will be expected to have more in-depth knowledge in your functional area. For example, if you are interested in business development, your depth of strategy knowledge should go well beyond the advanced beginner level if you are to land a job in that field. The company that hires you for a business development role does so because it believes that you can make immediate and sustained contributions to the organization. While companies generally expect their new MBA hires to display competence in their primary functional area, one potential exception to this is career switchers who are pursuing a field that is different from the one they worked in before business school. Companies know that the business school timeline is short, requiring you to secure an internship while you are still taking your core MBA courses.

As a career switcher, having an advanced beginner knowledge base, even in your primary functional area, is likely enough to secure an internship in that field. While building your knowledge, it will be important to develop a strong industry context by conducting thorough research and talking with industry insiders. Let's say, for example, that you worked in education before and have decided to transition into marketing after business school. As you go through your first-year marketing class, you will begin to develop a strong foundation in marketing concepts, from the 4 P's of product, price, place, and promotion to product life cycles. Beyond the classroom, you will learn more about brand management and the consumer packaged goods industry through research and conversations with students and alumni who are experienced in the industry. When General Mills or PepsiCo interviews you, the company will expect that you can apply fundamental marketing concepts and display a genuine interest in the field. With no marketing background, companies will not expect you to have the expertise to design a successful multimillion-dollar marketing campaign.

SPECIALIZATION

While advanced beginner know-how may be enough to land an internship, your proficiency level in your functional area should be competent enough to get a full-time job. The knowledge you have at this level allows you to really understand what information is relevant to make accurate, well-thought-out decisions. There are two primary ways to become competent in a subject area: experience and extensive study. Of course, an internship will provide you with valuable experience. You will be in marketing meetings and will work on projects that bring to life the abstract concepts that you learned in class. You can also develop competence in an academic setting. Take the marketing research specialization at the University of Wisconsin MBA program. With courses such as Qualitative-Based Marketing Insights, Marketing Research, and Quantitative Models in Marketing, extensive study can position you to be competent in the subject area.

With specializations, concentrations, and majors, you will have the opportunity for more rigorous study in a particular discipline. This could be in a functional area, such as organizational behavior, or at some schools may even be in an industry specialty, such as real estate or health care. But before you choose a specialty, consider your short-term and long-term aspirations. Do you want to advance in your current field? Or do you want to change fields? Are you looking to join or launch a start-up?

As you determine your specialty, you should develop a strong knowledge base to achieve your short-term goals and then turn your attention to what you will need to reach your long-term goals. If your short-term goal is a big switch from your previous experience, then your specialty in business school should be in that new area. If your goal is to advance in the same field where you have been employed, you can choose to deepen your knowledge further in that area, or you may choose to concentrate in another subject. If you choose the latter, then take your long-term goals into consideration. For example, if you are pursuing marketing positions immediately after school but intend to launch a business later in your career, then you might consider an entrepreneurship focus.

Most MBA programs will limit the number of classes that you can take in any one departmental area, such as organizational behavior or marketing. As always, you need to understand the requirements of your school. Schools will have specific requirements for a particular concentration or major, but you could always opt to loosely craft your own specialty, even if it would not be recognized as such by your school.

YOU, THE EXPERT

The final stop on the novice-expert knowledge continuum is clearly the expert. As an MBA, you should be an expert in something—eventually. The MBA itself is a general management degree, but as you progress in your career, you should develop a high level of expertise in at least one or two content areas. These could be broad or narrow topic areas, but you want to have the highest level of proficiency in something. You will never know everything about a topic, but with robust knowledge and insight gained through extensive study and developed through your experiences and with credentials built over time, your expertise will become almost intuitive.

In reality, with only 21 months of business school, you won't have time to become an expert in much of anything, but you can begin the journey. Even if you do develop into an expert in one area, what about every other subject? You can't possibly learn it all. You don't have time. Alas, better than being an expert is knowing lots of different experts. Queue up the Beatles' "I Get By with a Little Help from My Friends." You will find experts all around your business school, especially among the faculty and alumni network. And never forget that expertise comes in all shapes and sizes. Maybe you want to work in private wealth management, and one of your classmates just left Goldman Sachs. While she was only a junior analyst at the firm, she may be an expert on Goldman Sachs culture and politics and navigating the interview process. Take advantage of her knowledge and make it your own.

When you acknowledge that you need experts in your network, you will more proactively look for them, and you will begin to recognize all sorts of expertise that other people have. Then you can add them to your network too. In my case, I am always looking for marketing experts. My aversion to marketing was actually crystallized in business school. It was the worst class I took at Darden (and I'm not ashamed to say that marketing was my worst grade in grad school, and I think I deserve my money back for that class). I get the subject—I'm competent—but at the same time, I really don't get it. I don't have much interest in marketing, although over the years I haven't been able to hide from it. So instead of faking it, I call on my friends who are marketing experts. Now, I didn't just befriend them for their marketing knowledge, but it does come in handy when I need some help. Build a circle of colleagues and friends who have knowledge that you need.

Classroom. It should be abundantly clear by now that the classroom experience is the foundation for building your knowledge. Many of the classes that you will take, at least initially, will be required courses and will give you breadth in your general management knowledge base. As you are able to make course choices, think about the depth of the knowledge that you want to develop. Determine in what areas you many want to become expert in the future and in what subjects you want to become competent now.

By your second year, fatigue will start to set in. Continue to push yourself to take the classes that will benefit your career short-term and long-term. Pick elective courses not just based on subject matter but also on teacher quality. You can absorb information by reading a book, but with an excellent professor, you will be more engaged and will learn and retain more. It is tempting to avoid risk and stick with less challenging professors and less demanding courses, but that is not why you are in business school. So, take some chances. Find at least one or two classes that will really push you and prepare you to reach your goals.

While we have spent much of this chapter addressing information and knowledge gathering, expertise is achieved more quickly through applying that knowledge. The most readily available way for doing this is to speak up in class. Yes! Step out from the books and the research and start talking. This means making statements and asserting positions. Sometimes you will be right. Other times you will be wrong. Either way, you will synthesize information quickly and will become more comfortable with the topic. If you are to master a subject, then silence in class is not an option.

I have found that for many women, speaking up in class, particularly when they aren't confident in the concepts or how to apply them, is downright frightening and is thus avoided at all costs. It is difficult for many women to jump into the fray. If you put yourself in this category, you must challenge yourself to speak up. The more you do so, the more your knowledge base will improve (as will your communication skills).

In addition to speaking up in class regarding what you know or think you know, share your insights with those who know less than you. When you are teaching a concept to someone else and having to break it down in different ways, you grasp the concept even better. So, don't be shy about helping others learn what you know. The reverse of this is also true: don't be shy about asking for help. You don't have to figure it all out by yourself. You will get the answer more quickly, and just as important, you will get in the habit of asking for help, which you will have to do just about every day for the rest of your career.

As you get help, leverage your professors. It is actually their job to teach you the concepts. Talk with them after class or visit them during office hours. Remember, you are building your knowledge, and professors have tons of it. The added benefit is that your professor will see that you are inquisitive and engaged in the class. While you will be asking questions about what you don't know, what you *do* know will shine through, and in the end this will not only impact your learning but may also improve your grade.

Career. As you develop knowledge and expertise for your career and industry pursuits, determine who has the information that you want and need. Consider alumni and professionals who work at your companies of interest, along with the second-year students who interned at those companies. Other sources of information include any students who have experience in the industry generally and the career services office. Make sure you are gathering industry and topical information that helps you master the underlying concepts and knowledge. All too often, MBA students are too focused on the process of getting a job, such as how to get selected for an interview or ways to improve their interview skills. Of course this is critical insight, but before you hone in on what you need to say and how you need to say it, learn the underlying information.

If you are interested in working at Google or Amazon, prioritize building your expertise on the technology industry, on innovation, on product development, or on how consumer insights and the industry continue to evolve. This knowledge will carry you much further as you prepare for internship interviews and also for success on the job. Remember that when you are developing your knowledge and expertise, you are also strengthening your product and personal brand.

As with the classroom, extensive study to develop knowledge is useful, but presenting the information to others will really help you figure out what you know and where more study is required. Attend corporate events, receptions, and campus information sessions. Companies host these so that they can identify potential interns and employees and sell you on their organizations and the opportunities that they offer. Often they bring a senior leader from the organization to make remarks and allow for students to ask questions, then they break for networking among the students and company representatives. Having been a recruiter, I find that whenever there is a question-and-answer session, men go crazy asking questions, while women tend to be a bit more reserved, often saving their questions until the networking portion of the event.

Not every question needs to be asked in front of the whole audience—I wish someone would let our male counterparts know that—but make sure that when you do have a question you don't shy away from asking it. This is a loss for you and for your fellow classmates. In the spirit of developing knowledge and sharing it, I want you to consider doing the following at corporate information sessions. First, prepare for the event. Research the company and the representatives who will be attending. Make sure that you are staying up on current events at the company and on competitors and general industry information. As you get close to the event, write down a few questions about the industry, the company, and opportunities within the organization. Then before attending the event, set specific goals that you want to attain. For example:

- I will make two new professional contacts who work in the division where I want to work (one of whom seems open to helping me further understand the nuances of the industry and the company).

- During the networking portion, beyond asking questions, I will make one industry- or company-specific comment during the conversation to test what I've been learning.
- I will ask a question of the main speaker during the question-and-answer session.

You may not feel comfortable trying this all at your first information session, but work your way up. Challenge yourself by testing your knowledge, asking meaningful and thoughtful questions, and making comments that showcase your competence on the subject matter.

In addition to the general events, several companies offer events that specifically target women. These tend to be more intimate events, so they are ideal for knowledge building. One thing I don't like about these events is that they often focus too much on the culture of the firm or on how women navigate politics and other issues in the firm. These very important topics will certainly help you select the right company, but in the first semester of business school, they are at best good-to-know insights. You are trying to get the internship and figure out how to do well in it. When you are in these sessions, focus on the must-know stuff that will help you achieve a competent level of functional and industry knowledge. If you find yourself in conversations that are veering too far from knowledge building, ask a question to get the conversation back on track, such as "How do you expect the industry to change in light of [some recent development]?" As you become confident in your emerging expertise, then feel free to focus your attention more on the culture of your target companies and on understanding the experiences of women and others at the firms to determine the place that is the best fit for you.

Clubs. Clubs can be an awesome source for developing your knowledge and expertise. Club meetings and events, such as conferences, treks, and training sessions, offer you access to people who are interested in and studying the same subjects. In your first semester you will have to do very little work, because the second-year students do most of the planning and execution of club activities. You just need to show up, participate, and be an active learner. As you are gaining value, let your peers know so that they can benefit as well.

When possible, take advantage of clubs that provide not only information but also hands-on experience, particularly when you are new to a field. This can really bring the subject matter to life and allow you to apply the concepts that you are learning. For example, at the UCLA Anderson School of Management, you could be one of the students selected to participate in the Student Investment Fund in which you will not only learn about investment theory but will also manage a real portfolio of more than $2 million! Just about every top business school has an entrepreneurship club in which you can network with successful entrepreneurs or work with local entrepreneurs, helping them grow their businesses. These clubs aren't just a way to fatten up your résumé, although they will do that. They also help you build the knowledge and hands-on experiences that will support you in achieving your professional goals.

Community. When I was in school, I realized that when men, particularly MBA men, talk to each other, they pretty seamlessly move their conversation from professional topics to sports to random crap and back to professional topics again. Even when they're drinking heavily, don't be surprised to hear business talk. Guys have totally mastered professional small talk, especially with each other. This must be some male rite of passage that they fulfilled and we women somehow missed. Now, of course, women know how to make small talk, but when we start a professional conversation, we either keep it professional the whole time or, when it does move into the personal, casual realm, it is definitely not going back to the business talk, especially when drinking is involved.

Inherently there is nothing wrong with this. Clearly, we are better at unwinding! But in the context of building knowledge, even in seemingly social settings, women need to focus more on business. These conversations may not be where the actual knowledge building occurs, but they may serve as the vehicle for forming a personal connection to facilitate access to experts down the road. This is particularly true of your interactions with professors during school-sponsored social events. You might run into a professor at a school food festival on a Friday night. Business professors live for this semi-professional networking with students. Approach them. Doing so at social events should be far less intimidating than in the classroom, and the more you engage in such social interaction, the more confidence you will bring to the professional environment.

There is so much professional power in community. When we draw a solid line between business conversations and hanging-out time, we may miss opportunities. Often the closest professional relationships that people have started with some social or more casual interaction. So, make a mental list of your friends and acquaintances, and then consider who on that list may have information and experience that will help you obtain deeper knowledge in your field.

Personal investing. I have one final thought on building your knowledge in business school, and this is a bit of a digression—sue me. I believe that the MBA is such an awesome degree because of its flexibility. You have one main educational requirement—become a competent general manager by developing at least advanced beginner–level expertise in each of the core business subjects. While advanced beginner is fine in corporate finance, it is not enough in personal finance. Now, business schools don't generally teach personal finance and investing. But as an MBA, you must be a competent personal investor and money manager.

If you are going to manage other people's assets (you will likely have some budget responsibility), then you need to effectively manage your own assets. As women, personal investing is critical. Women make less money over their careers and live longer than men, yet we invest less. This impacts not only our retirement nest egg but also our ability to invest in our own businesses and other ventures. A 2011 Hearts & Wallets survey found that 41 percent of women felt that they were inexperienced with investing, as compared to only 27 percent of men.[1]

The upside is that when we do invest, not surprising to me, we outperform men. According to the *Chicago Tribune,* Brad Barber, professor of finance at the University of California at Davis and coauthor of the study *Boys Will Be Boys: Gender, Overconfidence and Common Stock Investment,* found that men traded stocks twice as often as women, yet women's portfolios tended to outperform men's.

Personal investing is about more than deciding what stocks and bonds to buy or sell; it is also about an approach to building your wealth. Too many MBAs are always looking to make more money instead of looking for ways to make the money they already have work for them. When they make more money, they upgrade their lifestyles accordingly, and their bank accounts look as paltry as they did before. This leaves them in the same exact position that they were in before they got the degree, the job, or the promotion. Yes, you want to live life well, but having money means having choices, such as being able to take a pay cut to pursue a new goal. This is a luxury that every MBA, especially from a top school, should have.

There will likely not be many business school classes on personal investing, but there are lots of books and websites on money management that you can study. Also stay close to your friends who are pursuing private wealth management and learn from them. You are an MBA. You should and can understand how money is managed, and you should not be afraid of investing to build your financial wealth.

JARGON ALERT

Commoditize. Having one's product or service widely available and interchangeable with that of another company.

Core competencies. What a company does best. Or thinks it does.

End-to-end. An adjective that means from the front end, facing the customer, to your company's back office.

REVIEW: THE SHORT, SHORT VERSION

- Your MBA is a general management degree that unlocks many different doors.
- Before you choose a specialty, consider your short-term and long-term goals.
- In the classroom, pick elective courses based not just on subject matter but also on the quality of the professor.
- Speak out and be visible. Get out of your comfort zone.
- Clubs that align with your short-term goals will help you develop your industry knowledge and expertise. You can also use your social time in business school to build your knowledge.
- You don't have to be an overnight expert. Instead, know and learn from lots of experts.
- Women live longer than men and don't invest as much. Prioritize personal investing and money management.

In business school, you will have an opportunity to challenge yourself in an environment with relatively low risk. In the next chapter, you will learn how to assess your skills and decide which ones you need to work on.

11

Take Shots on the Practice Range
Developing Skills and Experience for the Real World

During my career, I have worked in corporate, academia, nonprofit, and start-up environments. My job titles have included corporate finance associate, associate director, recruiter, program director, vice president, and executive director. In each of these organizations and roles, I had to acquire lots of new knowledge and relationships. Being inquisitive and connecting with key stakeholders were important to my success. Yet, it was my skill set that ultimately dictated my ability to excel in every job for which I was hired. As you build your MBA assets to catapult your professional career, it is important to improve your subject-matter expertise and cultivate powerful relationships. Also develop and strengthen your skills, which will in large part drive your on-the-job performance.

Your skills help you get things done. Carolyn Miles, president and CEO of Save the Children and a fellow Darden alumna, explained that organizations will hire you expecting you to add value right away. She said that in her career, which has spanned the private and nonprofit sectors with both domestic and international assignments, she always had this "core set of competencies that I could kind of hang on to and take with me." As you project out to your first post-MBA job and then your second and your third, what will be the skills that you need to develop and take with you that enable you to get things done?

Business school isn't necessarily the setting for learning lots of new skills—the urgency of class, career, and club and community activities is overwhelming, making it difficult to prioritize developing a brand new skill. You already possess so many important skills, though, such as communication and analytical skills—you can't get into a top MBA program without them. Business school offers you a relatively safe setting to strengthen, enhance, and practice many of the skills that you already have.

My approach to skill development is simple. First, excellence trumps mediocrity. Second, skills are learned, not innate. Of course, being great at something is better than being average at it. That's not what I mean here. Being the best at certain essential skills compensates for other skills in which you are not as strong. Superstar employees advance in their organizations based on their strengths, not based on having no weaknesses. Your excellence in certain skills trumps your mediocrity in others. You want to address glaring gaps in your skill set, but beyond that, focus on nurturing your strengths or the skills that can become your strengths.

When we observe someone who outshines others in a particular area, we readily assume that she is a natural. This assumption minimizes the effort that she put in to building her strengths and also lessens our own belief and resolve that we can develop a particular skill so that it becomes one of our strengths. I'm not suggesting that you can or will be the best at every skill you possess, but I am saying that you have tremendous control over your skill development. Skills are learned abilities developed through training, practice, and experience.

ASSESS YOUR SKILLS

It is important to know where you stand—knowing what you do well and what you don't do well and determining in what ways you can improve. Make a list of all of the skills that you deem important, capturing those that are relevant to your aspirations and those that may relate to your ego and personal brand. Be as comprehensive as possible, even including skills that may not be directly related to your current professional aspirations. Interpersonal, analytical, professional, and written communication skills are examples. You may also want to drill down into more specifics. For example, with analytical skills, if you are interested in equity capital markets, you might include valuation and financial modeling. Or if you are interested in management consulting, you might include structured problem solving and data analysis.

Once you have your list of skills, rate the relevance of each to your career aspirations. Is it an essential skill? For example, if you are interested in technology product development and innovation, then strategic planning, analytical, and project management skills would be highly relevant to your success in the field. Public speaking and quantitative skills might be somewhat relevant to your aspirations, while event management may not be particularly relevant.

Next, rate your mastery of each skill on your list. You are trying to get a baseline understanding of where you stand. Are you excellent, above average, average, or below average? Put an asterisk next to any skill in which you are not currently excellent but believe that you have the strong potential to be such. Don't be overly critical. I have found—and studies bear this out—that women tend to more harshly assess themselves than men do. In fact, when I lead training sessions and ask participants to rate themselves on a scale of 1 to 10, I always follow that up with "ladies, add at least 1 point to your rating, and men, subtract a point" to account for this phenomenon and get closer to the real number.

Draw a circle around the skills for which you rated your mastery at above average or excellent and that are highly relevant. These are likely strengths that you use consistently to get things done and that others rely on you to deliver. If they are not central to your personal brand, consider how to incorporate them. You want to highlight these skills in your résumé and when you talk about yourself and your capabilities. You also want to find new opportunities for using these skills—showcasing them for others and practicing them for continuous improvement. Remember, your aim is to be the best in these areas.

Draw a box around the skills for which you rated your mastery at below average and that are highly relevant. These skills and your lack of confidence in your mastery of them are likely the source of a little anxiety. No worries! Remember that skills are learned, not inherited, so you can improve at least to average proficiency. You may never be known as an expert in this area, but it shouldn't be your fatal flaw either. Caveat: if the majority of the skills you listed as highly relevant have a box around them instead of circle, then either you are being too hard on yourself and need a rate adjustment or you need to reevaluate whether your career aspirations really align with your ego.

DEVELOP YOUR SKILLS

Regardless of your career path, there are many skills that you will be required to exhibit, such as time management, organizational, and interpersonal skills. While you will ultimately decide where to focus your efforts while in business school, I want to spend the remainder of this chapter discussing the essential skills that are particularly well situated for development in business school. Business school is a relatively low-risk setting for practicing these skills—you are in a learning environment where people more often than not are very willing to help you, and there are lots of opportunities for feedback and support. Of course, there are some risks, including two big ones: your reputation and your confidence. But now is the time, outside of the employer-employee structure, to practice and prepare for the higher-stakes management roles that you will have in the future. Furthermore, you won't be the only one trying out new things—you are surrounded by classmates who are practicing their skills, too.

There are four essential skills: relationship management, analytical, communication, and negotiation skills. We will cover relationship management separately in the next chapter and address the other three skills here. These four essential skills are universally important, so being below average in any of them may be detrimental to your career progression. On the other hand, if you can develop one or more to levels of excellence, you will have the power to harness them for career success.

There are entire books written about each of these essential skills, so we'll address some of the gender-specific opportunities that you will have to practice and display these skills while in business school. This is based not only on well-researched gender norms but also on my own experience and the anecdotal evidence from the many subjects I interviewed in writing this book.

ANALYTICAL SKILLS

Many women have had a lifetime of subtle and overt messages and experiences that have reinforced an erroneous myth that women are not as strong as men in math and quantitative subjects. This is simply not true but still manifests itself in the professional world and throughout most levels of education, even in graduate business schools. Regardless of whether or not you enjoyed calculus when you took it in high school, you can develop robust analytical skills that will be invaluable in your professional career.

In a nutshell, strong analytical skills enable you to recognize and process a problem, concept, or situation and identify issues, interdependencies, and options for developing solutions and making logical decisions. Though often used interchangeably with the term "analytical skills," quantitative skills involve the actual math, computations, and calculations. Analytical skills involve the theory behind the numbers. While they are closely related, analytical skills are much broader than quantitative skills. Analytical skills are displayed through problem solving, research, and project management and are not all about numbers. Analytical skills are required in any post-MBA position. You will use them constantly, from leading a strategic planning meeting with your team to completing your assignments, managing others, and making decisions.

We often think that the best analytical thinkers are engineers or those in highly technical fields, but there are many disciplines with well-developed analytical skills. For example, college liberal arts programs are specifically designed to develop students' analytical skills to deal with a complex and changing world. Consider your work and education where, for instance, you have used your critical thinking and reasoning or had to process information to prove an argument. History majors are just as likely as computer science majors to use this skill.

You got yourself admitted to business school, so you at least have basic analytical skills (you performed adequately enough on the GMAT); now it is time to take them to the next level.

To develop any skill, you need training, practice, and experience. While you won't find a business school course called Analysis designed solely to teach you to analyze different problems, most courses offer some instruction on the subject. In accounting, if it is taught well, you will not only learn the rules of financial statements and how financial information is reported but will also learn how to analyze that information to make better decisions. In this and your other classes, you will receive more than enough theories and frameworks for analyzing management issues and business opportunities.

As a graduate student, you are more likely to have a vested interest in learning the material so that you can apply it in your career. With that said, the pace and volume of the course work, along with the other time-consuming aspects of business school, often lead MBA students to learn just enough to complete their assignments and pass the test. This is particularly true when the course is not directly related to their professional interests. Resolve instead to study analysis and structured problem solving in every subject, breaking down the complex problems and topics covered to get a better understanding of them. Engage your professors and your classmates to explain things that you don't understand and to help you figure out how it all fits together. Apply the same learning principles to your club engagement and career exploration. For example, the consulting industry is recognized for structured problem solving. So, you might take advantage of a session on analyzing a case, a typical format for consulting job interviews, offered by a student-led consulting club or management consulting firm.

As you are learning to analyze problems, practice the skill as well. If you are in study groups, take the lead on assignments that require complex problem solving. Select student clubs that enable you to strengthen your structured analytical skills. For example, at Chicago Booth you could participate in valuation and modeling seminars offered by the Investment Banking Group. If you are interested in entrepreneurship, at Cornell Johnson you can serve local businesses by analyzing issues and devising solutions, thus helping them meet their business objectives. Or you might participate in a case competition, such as the Human Resources Case Competition at Vanderbilt Owen Graduate School of Business sponsored by Deloitte Consulting.

One of the best ways to learn is by observing others. At a school social, you may find yourself talking with a professor and a few classmates about a current event. How are others analyzing the situation? What are the assumptions that they are making? How are they arriving at their conclusions? While it is great to observe, don't be a silent observer. Just as we discussed with regard to knowledge in the last chapter, your analytical skills are best practiced out loud. Your natural instinct might be to hunker down in your apartment with books on analytical skills, to pour yourself privately into your finance and statistics assignments, or to hopefully just get it through osmosis, but fight this temptation mightily. Instead, focus on getting the analysis out of your head and out of your mouth. This will allow others to give you feedback and push your reasoning.

In the classroom and in career activities in particular, women too often take the silent-observer role. In the classroom, men generally talk more than women—a lot more.[1] This is especially true when the subject area is one in which women feel less comfortable. A huge part of practicing your analytical skills is effectively conveying your thought process and your conclusions—out loud to others!

During class discussions, add your perspective on the topics that you know, and as you get more comfortable, begin to chime in on subjects on which you are less sure. While men talk more in class, the goal here is not to copy them. Women tend to listen and deliberate more, which can lead to more thoughtful responses, but you actually have to get into the conversation so that those comments can be shared. You may be the person who listens and then you have an idea, but by the time you raise your hand, the conversation has turned to something else. Don't feel like you can't go back if something hasn't been shared; add to the dialogue by providing new information and asking questions that may uncover assumptions or holes in the logic.

Also, don't hesitate to ask questions, which is part of analyzing and assessing what you are hearing. This is another way to distinguish yourself, but be prepared to give your opinion or explain why you have the question. This also applies to your interactions with potential employers. As you are preparing for corporate presentations and information sessions, analyze current market events and company data to devise questions that you might ask of the company representatives. Engage them in discussions by not simply asking them your well-crafted questions but also by conveying your observations and conclusions.

As your experience in analyzing issues increases, so will your confidence and mastery of the skill. For some women, in the midst of a conversation, particularly when on the hot seat, it is hard to analyze and process information in the moment. We've all had the temporary brain freeze when our mind goes blank and we get stuck. Practicing will help to reduce the angst. But also know that when analyzing just about anything, you will never have perfect information. You will always have to deal with ambiguity or incomplete or imperfect information, so you have to make the best guess based on what you do know and communicate your reasoning. Expect that others will challenge or have questions about your approach, which may then require you to further support your position.

COMMUNICATION SKILLS

Your analysis is only as effective as your ability to convey it, so you must communicate in a way that allows others to hear what you are saying. Daria Torres, managing partner of Walls Torres Group LLC and adjunct faculty member at the Wharton School of the University of Pennsylvania and the Rutgers University School of Business, says that being heard is really tied to your ability to project authority. She explains that the ability to project authority is governed by your level of confidence and your sense of entitlement to speak, to object, or to be wrong. Consider when you've been in a meeting in which you assertively shared your comments and challenged ideas in the spirit of open dialogue. You were confident in yourself and the knowledge and insight you were bringing to the conversation, and thus you felt entitled or authorized to participate fully. The reverse of this situation, when someone is unable to project authority, is fueled by self-doubt, which breeds fear and in essence a need for permission to speak, to object, or to be wrong. Consider a meeting where you didn't speak up even though you had information that would have benefited the person or group. Why did you remain silent? Was it that you were unsure of yourself or your ability to communicate the information well? Were you unsure that you were allowed to speak or worried that no one would value your comments?

Although your confidence and entitlement to speak drive your ability to project authority in your communication, you don't actually have to develop confidence and entitlement first. Torres suggests experimenting with tactics that you know display gravitas and influence. Then gauge the results, and if they are positive, replicate the behavior until it becomes habitual or natural. Ann Cuddy, Harvard Business School professor, puts it another way: "Fake it until you become it."

So, what are the best tactics? The key is to test out different behaviors and approaches to determine what works for you. As you use them in your communication, you will feel others gravitating toward your authority. Here are some ways to do that.

Cut to the chase. Start with your thesis. Many women are not linear thinkers and direct communicators. Seeing multiple facets of any issues, there is often a desire to explain the nuance. Don't limit your creative and more expansive deliberation, but do remember that not everyone approaches issues in the same way. When sharing your insights, particularly when you have limited air time, start with the solution and then explain how you got there. Even when you are thinking out loud, start with the end in mind.

Make direct versus indirect statements. Don't say "I'd like to talk about this project." Instead say "We need to change the scope of this project." Women feel better receiving indirect communication, and that is why we give it. Sometimes, especially in personal situations, this is often the right tactic, but as a rule in professional settings, it is best to start with a direct statement and then explain the reasons for your decision.

Get rid of indecisive speech. Nix the rambling, long sentences that are telltale signs of apprehension, doubt, or not knowing whether you've made yourself clear. Limit uncertain qualifiers such as "a bit," "kind of," and "I guess." Also avoid tag questions at the end of a statement, such as "It's the best approach, isn't it?" This takes the authority way from what you have just communicated.

Speak up. Keep your voice clear and loud enough for everyone to hear you. Confidence is tied to the volume and tension of your voice. Take your time, breathe (from your diaphragm), and project your voice.

Practice keeping the tone of your voice level. Often our voices become high-pitched when we get anxious or nervous. Work to keep the tone of your voice low.

Avoid passive language. "Additional information could not be obtained." "Your cooperation in this matter is appreciated." What's wrong with these statements? There is no responsible person there. *Who* couldn't obtain additional information? *Who* will appreciate cooperation in the matter? If it is you, the speaker, say so.

Don't apologize. Maybe you don't have all the answers. Words are crude tools, but they are the best tools we have. Make your statement with the authority and passion that you feel. Don't qualify it, and never apologize (unless the purpose of your comments is actually to apologize).

From your body language to the words that you use, act and speak in ways that you believe project importance and confidence. Over time, this will actually increase your confidence and your feeling that you are entitled to fully participate in the conversation.

You will have lots of opportunities to practice communicating with authority in business school. It is critical that you become skilled at making assertive, clear statements that other people can understand when you are not the expert or are addressing people with a greater level of expertise or when you are in larger groups (such as in a classroom or at a corporate presentation) or when you are leading a club meeting.

An assertive speaker is a confident speaker. This person can state opinions and emotions clearly and make her case without violating anyone else's rights. She has excellent eye contact, uses "I" statements, and listens well without interrupting other speakers. Unlike aggressive or passive-aggressive speakers, the assertive speaker shows that she respects the opinions of others.

Your goal is to be an assertive speaker in order to increase your credibility and get the results that you intend. You might be trying to get people to agree with your point. You might be trying to get your study group to do something you want them to do. Or you might want a job or a second interview. An assertive speech style can get people to move in your favor.

For women, it can often be difficult to find the line between being assertive and begin aggressive, particularly when you feel like someone else is not listening to you or does not understand the points you are trying to convey. Let's just get it out there—we fear that we will be labeled as bitches. Frankly, we just have to get over that. Your focus has to be on getting your point across. Don't worry about other people's baggage. You won't be able to get your ideas on the table if you are afraid of how people are going to label you. Be an assertive speaker, and over time you will gain more supporters than enemies.

We have all experienced being passed over and ignored. And you are likely to experience this again when you get in an MBA classroom or when you are networking at a recruiting event. It is frustrating to make a point and then hear it praised 20 minutes later once a male in the classroom expresses that same thing. Don't agonize over it, and don't get bogged down. Move on, pushing yourself to come up with other arguments to strengthen your position.

If your comment gets glossed over and you think that the class is missing something, raise your hand again. Say "Can we come back to this comment?" or "I'd like to go further with that statement." Letting that one comment ride may not be enough. You may have to raise your hand and get back in there. Be assertive.

As you begin to make more comments in class, seek out feedback from a classmate or possibly even from the professor. Let your peer know before class that you are working to improve your class participation and want her to give you feedback on any comments you make. After class, find out if your comments were effective, if you appeared confident and assertive, and if she thought that others in the class understood your points.

The classroom experience is your opportunity to get used to talking about topics that you are not especially knowledgeable in. Uncomfortable as it may be, it is something that you must master, and the classroom is a pretty safe space in which to practice. As you continue to make assertive statements, you will become more confident in your thought processes and your ideas. Inevitably, sometimes you will be completely wrong. You must get comfortable with this reality too so that you can keep moving forward.

NEGOTIATION SKILLS

The unsettling feeling of being wrong is similar to the feeling that you have when you ask for something and don't get it—maybe this is one reason that women are less likely to ask for exactly what they want. And this brings us to the skill of negotiation. One of my business school regrets is that I didn't take the still-legendary Darden course, Bargaining & Negotiating. I had my reasons—the class didn't fit well into my already hectic JD/MBA schedule. In hindsight, though, it would have been worth the longer class day and figuring out what else I could have skipped or moved to accommodate the class.

I hadn't thought much about women and negotiating before writing this book. I carried many of the stereotypes and assumptions about negotiation that you may have. Women don't like to negotiate. Women are weaker negotiators. Of course, these are all in comparison to men. Now you might be thinking, *I don't negotiate much; when I do negotiate I don't like it, and I don't think I'm very good at it.* So, those aren't stereotypes—they are truisms. Women tend to find negotiation a bit distasteful, maybe because the agreement was less than we wanted or felt we deserved. Perhaps the process didn't feel good, a relationship was strained, or later what we had initially agreed to didn't come to pass. We may feel as if our likability is at stake if we negotiate too vigorously (and it well may be). We may not know that in a particular situation we can and should negotiate. And even when we know that we should negotiate, we may lack the tools, frameworks, and practice to do so effectively.

Negotiation is a critical skill for obvious reasons, such as negotiating compensation for a new job or terms for a business deal. But negotiation is truly a part of our everyday lives. In our homes, we negotiate distribution of housework and familial responsibilities. In our personal business dealings, we negotiate getting a contractor to increase what he or she provides without increasing the cost or getting a contractor to lower a price and deliver the same service. At work, we negotiate roles and responsibilities.

As I was writing this book, I was lucky enough to sit down with Darden professor Sherwood Frey, who taught my first-year Quantitative Analysis course and was also one of the bargaining and negotiating professors. I wish I could share everything that he told me in our conversation, but this would be a really long chapter! He shared one framework—"3 Ps and 3 Cs"—that I found particularly powerful and that I have used consistently since learning about it. The 3 Ps are prepare, probe, and propose, and the 3 Cs are create, claim, and close.

Prepare. Before you enter a negotiation, understand the situation and determine what you want and need. Gather research, historical data, and background information. Also consider the same information from your counterparty's perspective—how might your counterparty view the situation differently than you?

Probe. When you talk with your counterparty, find out what he or she wants and how that person is thinking about the situation. While your preparation for understanding your counterparty's perspective was speculation, here you are getting the real information. Listen carefully for differences in approach and to clarify any assumptions that you may have made.

Propose. Ask. In negotiation there is give and take, so with your initial offer push the envelope of reasonability. Asking is a huge first step, but it is not enough. You must stick with it. Don't fold when questioned about your initial offer. If you do, you will quickly lose your leverage.

Create. Increase the mutual value of the deal. Don't be limited by the initial offers. If you are able to exploit your differences, you can grow the overall value for both parties. Imagine that if you are simply focused on getting more than your counterparty, you might be satisfied to get 75 percent of the pie. But what if you could grow the pie to a point where you got 50 percent of an even larger pie that generated an absolute value that was higher than 75 percent of the smaller pie? Clearly you would be better off.

Claim. Work through the negotiation with your counterparty to reach a deal. Consciously remind yourself of what you hope to get from the deal. Set aggressive goals for the negotiation, not just the outcomes that you want but also how you want the negotiation process to go and how you want relationships to develop.

Close. Once the negotiation is done, frame the negotiation outcomes so that the counterparty knows that he or she has a good deal. Remind the counterparty of the value that he or she is receiving—you want the person to feel great about the outcome.

This is the crux of the negotiation, and there are in fact several things that women do well, particularly probing, creating mutual value, and closing so that the other party feels good about the deal. We are missing an opportunity around proposing and claiming, which largely draws on the same approach. In a nutshell, if you don't ask for it, you won't get it. You must push the envelope of reasonability, be aggressive (this is the time to be aggressive or at least highly assertive) with a rational approach, and stick to it. As you make the initial offer and subsequent counteroffers, you must believe that you deserve a great outcome.

As you go through the proposing and claiming process, consider ways to extend your fundamental approach. Sherwood says that generally we are either fundamentally cooperative or competitive. I tend to be cooperative in negotiation, so it makes sense that I might have an aversion to the process if I equate it with competition. Instead of trying to shift my approach to a competition stance, Sherwood suggested that I become "competitively cooperative" by slowing down on giving concessions and accepting the other party's terms. On the other hand, if you are a more competitive person, focus on becoming "cooperatively competitive" by listening to what your counterparty is saying to identify ways to grow the pie. While it may lead to your counterparty getting more when your competitive nature may long for the counterparty to get the least amount possible, it can result in you getting even more overall.

With any negotiation, don't give without getting something in return. When you receive an offer from your counterparty, don't simply say "yes." Instead, consider what you want in return for accepting that particular term. "I might be able to give X, if I get Y." Prioritize what you want instead of simply settling for what you think you can get.

Finally, when the negotiation is done, you may not feel satisfied initially because you didn't get your initial offer. But remember, your initial offer was superaggressive. Consider what you would have been willing to take initially and compare that to what you ultimately got by following this process. It is likely that the process generated more value for you.

As I mentioned, negotiating is truly an everyday skill that will enable you to get want you want. For example, when you are part of a team or working as a group, you need to decide who is going to do what. Negotiate. Men tend to negotiate everything, and they don't even think of it that way. Too frequently in a group project when asked what they want to work on, women will often ask, "Well what do you want to do?"—putting it back on the other party. Or they might say, "It doesn't matter." Of course it matters. Use this as an opportunity to negotiate. Determine what you want to work on. Don't just settle for note-taking responsibilities. (One of my pet peeves is the expectation in many groups that women will take notes, because mysteriously no man has legible handwriting. Unless you want to take notes, don't be relegated to this role.) Consider your skills and how they can best be served in this group. Reflect on how working on specific parts of this project might help you develop a skill, knowledge, or a relationship. You can still be a good teammate and do what you want to do.

Women don't negotiate aggressively enough. This is why after MBA graduation, we make almost $5,000 less than our male counterparts. Don't let it happen to you. In addition to your post-MBA salary, you can negotiate work-related outcomes such as start date, terms, location, and benefits. It is important to practice negotiation in lower-stakes situations so that when you get to the most important negotiations, such as salary and compensation, you are comfortable and confident with your skills.

It is true that women tend to be more collaborative, and you know by now that I'm not suggesting that we should be more like men. We bring some really unique things to the table, such as trying to find the win-win in a situation. Women believe that there is enough to go around, and we don't just think of what we can get. We think instead of how to grow the pool to make it bigger for everyone. We just can't be afraid to ask for our share.

JARGON ALERT

Bandwidth. Staff or capacity to handle a project. "We don't have the bandwidth for that."

Boiling the ocean. Doing something in a lengthy, inefficient, and futile manner.

Granular. Getting down to minute details, not always a welcomed approach.

REVIEW: THE SHORT, SHORT VERSION

- You already have awesome skills or you wouldn't be in business school. This is your opportunity to assess and develop them.
- Companies that hire you expect that you will be able to add value right away.
- Leverage business school to strengthen your analytical, communication, and negotiation skills.

We are social creatures, and we can't operate in a vacuum. Next, we will examine how to leverage and manage relationships in business school.

12

Human Catapult
Managing Relationships to Propel You toward Your Goals

Every job that I have had came through a relationship—I have never found a position from a job posting or a help-wanted ad. Instead, I was connected to opportunities via a friend who shared a job for which he thought I would be a fit, a business school classmate who passed along my résumé to her Human Resources Department with a personal note, and a mentor who made an introduction to a key decision maker. And in two instances, hiring managers specifically targeted me for roles that they had open. Relationships have been the key driver in my ability to access opportunities. Of course, I had to do well once I was on the job, but I might not have had the opportunity at all without the support of someone in my network.

Over much of my early career even as I was clearly gaining immense professional benefits from the many relationships that I had, I had a fairly negative view of relationship management. Networking events seemed particularly inauthentic, with everyone trying to get face time with the most prominent person in the room. It reminded me of the way fans would exalt and basically stalk athletes when I was at the University of Connecticut for my undergraduate studies. Students would lose their minds when a basketball player walked into Wing Express for a bite to eat. Then at some point it hit me that the networking that I had such an aversion to was not real relationship building but instead was actually hero-worshiping. And it was okay to detest that. As I let go of my own issues, I acknowledged how important relationships had always been in my life and my career.

Regardless of the post-MBA industry or the profession you pursue, you will need to have people—a professional network—in your corner to help you along the way. For many women, building relationships that advance our career objectives just doesn't feel as natural as building personal friendships. Former secretary of state Madeleine Albright said in an interview with the *Wall Street Journal* that "I think women are really good at making friends and not good at networking."[1] That is certainly something that I have struggled with, particularly early in my career.

PROFESSIONAL FRIENDSHIPS

A lot of us carry images of the ideal relationship manager with traits that are more associated with the way that men build connections—no wonder we feel less comfortable with the practice. It seems to me that for women to be at their best, they should not adjust themselves to be more like men but instead should tweak their view of the ideal relationship manager to be more like women. In turn, this may lead us to think of professional relationships as being more like professional friendships. This allows us to apply the same principles and approaches that we use so effectively in our personal friendships for our professional benefit.

Women excel at creating connections, collaborating, and supporting others. Often the very qualities that make you a great friend in your personal life can help you to build important relationships in your professional life. It is about creating a context for relationship building that is a genuine representation of who you are. Relationship management is a skill that you have been developing for your entire life. If you are like many women, though, professional relationship building has often been taxing. Now as you prepare to embark on business school where relationship building is a way of life, it is time to reframe how you leverage connections to strengthen your MBA slingshot. Your connection with others will be critical to getting the support that you need and to developing meaningful bonds as you strive for your aspirations.

While you have built hundreds and maybe thousands of relationships, you may never have dissected how a relationship is formed. Relationship management has three stages—initiate, cultivate, and maintain—and with any professional connections that you make, it is important to be aware of where you are so you can take the most appropriate action to move to the next stage with that person.

INITIATE THE RELATIONSHIP

The starting point for any relationship is when you initiate contact. This is as simple as walking up to someone, introducing yourself, and carrying on a brief conversation. You are making a connection in an attempt to get the relationship started. The key to successfully initiating a relationship is making a strong first impression so that the other person wants to continue to build on what you've started. The personal brand that you convey and the content of your conversation drive that first impression, and the link between the two of you begins to grow.

Often the best way to engage someone in conversation is to ask her questions to get her talking about herself—generally, successful people feel comfortable talking about their backgrounds. This will enable you to learn more about the other person, but be mindful that you don't want the conversation to be one-sided—you want to share something about yourself or your views. Especially as you enter the business school setting, you should be able to succinctly introduce yourself, providing a brief overview of your background and your career goals—this is your informal 60-second pitch, or elevator pitch, about who you are. Within the first few weeks of school, this will roll off your tongue easily as you share the same information over and over again. Be aware of the follow-up questions that people ask you about your background so that you can tweak your introduction.

As you introduce yourself, the opening is always the same—you start with your name. You want to clearly articulate your name—it is *your* name. If you don't do this already, get in the habit of saying your first and last name, not just your first name. Women introduce themselves using only their first name quite often. I freely acknowledge that this is one of my pet peeves. It makes me think of a high school cheerleader, twirling her hair, head cocked to the side. "My name is Bambi." I was a high school cheerleader so nothing against that, but really, this is business school.

I'm not sure what drives so many of us to say only our first names. Maybe we don't want to be overly formal. Maybe it is because so many of us give up our last names when we get married and take on our husband's last name, so we don't value it in the same way. Whatever the reason, we have to get out of this habit. Now, clearly in certain casual settings saying only your first name is appropriate, but in a business setting (and that includes business school), it is important to say your first and last names.

When saying your name, speak slowly and clearly. Some of us have pretty typical American names, such as Nicole, that will be more widely recognized. But for those of you who have names that are less common and harder for someone to remember or pronounce, make sure that you enunciate. Take your time; maybe give the person something to associate with your name. If you like being called a nickname, share it, but don't feel like you have to create a nickname because your name is a little more complicated. It is your name. Help people to learn it versus having a nickname that you are not excited about.

Many of your early business school relationships will be initiated in the classroom. Just as you are sharing your name with others, you want to get to know the names of your classmates. For some people, remembering names, particularly when meeting lots of new people, is really challenging. Don't let that be an excuse. As you are learning everyone's name, try to discover at least one cool thing about each person. It can be as simple as where the person is from or what industry she or he worked in before business school. You want to be more than just a nameless face, and so do other people. Take the time to get to know your classmates and their names.

Relationships get initiated in formal and informal ways. In formal situations, you are introduced by someone else or you meet in a professional capacity, such as a job interview. In informal situations, you may simply strike up a conversation with a person sitting next to you. Most people easily initiate new relationships daily but may struggle with initiating more strategic relationships—those in which you believe you would receive some benefit now or in the future.

You may feel less comfortable establishing a relationship with someone senior to you or a classmate whom you hold in high esteem. You may question why that person would want to build a relationship with you and wonder what you have to offer in return. In these situations, you absolutely want to understand what you bring to the relationships and how you might be beneficial to other people. It is important, though, that you don't define value or benefit too narrowly. Most people love to talk about themselves and share their advice—if you listen and use that advice, this may be enough to benefit the adviser from her perspective. In other cases, the reciprocal benefit of the relationship comes years down the road. While in business school, you will experience the great kindness of MBA alumni and students. The reciprocal benefit may be that you pass on that generosity to others when you are an alumna.

CULTIVATE THE RELATIONSHIP

Initiating relationships is the easy part; cultivating relationships requires more work. You already have some connection or basis for the relationship, but it is not fully formed yet. You and the other person must both want it to move forward, and you are going to need to put energy toward that. At this stage you will try to take the relationship from an acquaintance to a peer, an associate, or maybe even a friend. The key to move from initiating to cultivating relationships is follow-up. We all have examples of making a strong initial connection with someone, getting his or her contact information but then not following up with an e-mail as we promised to do. You want to avoid that at all costs.

I imagine you know people (or maybe it is you) who seem to be natural networkers. They seem to know everyone and are great at connecting with new people. While there are certainly people who have a knack for it, relationship management is not a gift—it is a skill to be developed. When you look behind the curtain of these natural networkers, you are likely to find that they consistently cultivate new relationships. Maybe they immediately send follow-up notes or connect with their new contacts via LinkedIn. Determine how you will cultivate all of the new relationships that you will build in business school. Don't just expect that it will happen. Make it happen!

When you meet someone, purposefully seek that person out for a conversation the next time you are at the same event, invite the person for coffee, or otherwise cultivate the relationship. Solid relationships are built on more than coffee, though. They are built on mutual respect.

Be courteous. As you are building relationships, be courteous. Keep your word. If you have said that you will follow up on something, do it without having to be reminded. Get back to your contacts in a timely manner. Return telephone calls and e-mails. If you have a big "Taker" sign around your neck, you aren't going to last in any business relationship for long (and probably not in any personal one either).

Say "Thank you." Too many people don't.

Practice reciprocation. Consider what you can contribute to others while in business school. Maybe you will be able to offer other people your skills, your life experience, or industry expertise. Beyond this, you can also cultivate relationships by offering the intangibles that cause others to want to be around you, such as energy, enthusiasm, encouragement, and friendship.

Relationships are built one at a time, but you may find a pool of prospects you are interested in getting to know in a group that already exists. Then you can leverage the group's events and activities as you are cultivating individual relationships. In business school, the community is generally pretty open, and groups, both formal and informal, actively welcome new members. With that said, there are times when this will not the case. Once you determine who you want in your network, you may need to be aggressive in meeting people and breaking through cliques. Some of these cliques may be boys-only, and, yes, sometimes the boys will exclude you intentionally. Many times, however, they aren't trying to. They're just doing what they always do—getting together with guys with whom they think they have things in common. Don't let yourself be unintentionally excluded. If they mention that they went out for drinks, say, "Let me know next time, and I'll join you." If it is intentional, you will find that out in a hurry. Don't necessarily give up on engaging with the group—consider another approach. Maybe there is a ringleader who is pushing for exclusivity. Instead of trying to get in with him, focus on the other group members. Engage with those people who are open to you.

MAINTAIN THE RELATIONSHIP

You've probably heard the saying "It's not what you know, it's who you know." I think that this statement is incomplete and really should be "It's not who you know, but *what you do with* who you know." Relationships are built in the cultivation stage, but this last stage dictates whether that person says he or she knew you (past tense) or knows you (present tense). You want it to be present tense, and to achieve that you must maintain the relationship. Think about the great professional relationships that you developed over the years that have faded away, maybe a former manager, work colleagues, advisers, or recruiters. You did so much work to cultivate those relationships but didn't maintain them. Of course, there are cases in which you built such a strong relationship that being out of touch didn't reduce the affinity and connection that you have. But in many cases, you have stale contacts whom you wouldn't feel comfortable about contacting now. You may know that person, but you aren't in a position to do anything with that contact.

The duration of your relationships will vary, of course. Some will be short, and some may last a lifetime. You've done the hard work to cultivate the relationship, but sustaining a long-term relationship requires maintenance. To avoid losing the benefits of the relationships that you cultivate, you must post your contacts regularly—keeping them informed about what you are doing and where you are. This means periodic updates and check-ins. Consider developing a plan for maintaining your relationships—determine how you will track your contacts, how often you will be in touch, and in what manner you will correspond with your contacts. You may want to send a quarterly or annual update to friends and former coworkers. Basically, you're saying "I'm still out there. Here's how you can be supportive."

Staying in touch with your professional network with great care will strengthen these ties and build a pool of contacts whom you can call on down the road. For highly relevant contacts, reach out every other month. Put it on your calendar. If, for example, an alumnus was particularly helpful as you were going through the MBA application process, post that person on your progress during business school. Again, remember to thank the person for her or his support—thank you never gets old.

BUILDING RELATIONSHIPS IN BUSINESS SCHOOL

Each of the four channels—classroom experience, career exploration, club engagement, and community and social life—is designed to help you build robust relationships while you are in business school. So, your task is to determine the relationships that you want to build and the approach that you will take in building them. Consider who you want to be in your professional network 10 to 15 years after business school as well as who you may want to be in it 10 to 15 days after starting business school. Throughout this book we have touched on formal roles that people can play within your network. For example, in Chapter 1 we discussed how your MBA network can generate potential business partners, informers to provide you with business ideas or leads, and customers to buy products and services that you offer. And in the next chapter, we will cover the need for accountability partners, industry peers, industry insiders, mentors, sponsors, and backers.

You are capable of determining the specific relationships that you need. Don't just think about individual relationships; consider your network holistically. Make sure that you have a diverse cadre of relationships. As you engage with people on campus, seek out people from different backgrounds whom you might not usually befriend. Take a broad view of your ideal network. Although you want to key in on people whom you believe can help you, you never know who will make an introduction, give you a great insight, or just make you smile.

PERSONAL BOARD OF DIRECTORS

You already know that you must have a professional network, but consider specifically building your own personal board of directors. Even the most powerful executives of large companies seek guidance and direction from a board of directors. You should do the same. This group of advisers is basically a series of mentors. Instead of trying to find one perfect mentor, which will be impossible, you can create a board that will give you diversity in perspectives and backgrounds. As you grapple with job, career, and life decisions, your board can serve as a sounding board, provide valuable insight, and connect you to other people who may be helpful to you. There are various roles that you may want to fill on your board of directors. As you select your board, know that some directors may play more than one role, and they don't necessarily need to be senior to you.

Experts. These are industry insiders, functional experts, and industry experts. The more diverse your field of experts, the more diverse knowledge base that you have access to.

Connectors. These people may not be your end target themselves, but they can connect you to other professionals who are. Connectors may be business school professors, alumni, or friends who can help you connect with those you can't reach on your own. In addition to finding connectors to have in your circle, make an effort to be a connector to others when you can. This is one of the most effective ways to provide reciprocal benefit to a person who is helping you.

Encouragers. They know that you are wonderful, and they are happy to tell you and the rest of the world all about it. This isn't frivolous stuff. We need others to spread the word about us and enable our personal brand to go viral. Additionally, we all need people whose view of us makes us remember how awesome we are—especially on those days when we doubt ourselves. Your encouragers will do that for you.

Truth tellers. Just as the encouragers tell you that you can conquer the world, the truth tellers ask to see your action plan. Note that they are not naysayers. They are clear-headed, clear-eyed people who will ask you the right questions and identify potential pitfalls to help you increase your likelihood of success.

Strategic/big-picture thinkers. These people are the ones who can help you plan a path to get to where you want to go. They may also be truth tellers, encouragers, connectors, or experts, but their primary job will be to help you strategize.

Mountain movers. You want to have people in your network who are mountain movers—who make big things happen. They inspire you to see what is possible through their actions. This is the person who doesn't see challenges as insurmountable obstacles but instead sees them as unqualified opportunities to achieve more than you original planned.

Operatives. These are the people who get things done. They are often responsible for activities that in the scheme of our big important worlds seem relatively inconsequential—that is until we need them. The information technology help desks at business schools come to mind. They often go unnoticed until a laptop crash. You don't know when you're going to need someone's help. Actively seek out and befriend operatives, particularly in areas in which you lack expertise or know-how.

Skill modelers. These are people with specific skills and traits that you admire, such as strong communication or assertiveness. In some cases, you can watch and emulate what you see. In other cases, you will want to engage them to get some informal coaching on how you might develop your skill in a particular area.

Develop a board of directors that you are able to manage. Determine the number of high-touch mentor relationships that you can consistently maintain. You want to keep them all abreast of how you are doing, what is going well, and what you are struggling with. While your board is assembled to support you, you always want to present yourself in a manner that aligns with your personal brand.

My goal in this chapter has been to show you the stages of relationship management but, just as important, to help you see how important this skill is not just for business school but for your entire career. It is about engaging people and drawing them to you so they can help you achieve your goals. This is something we women can do really well. Start building!

JARGON ALERT

Dialogue. Used as a verb to mean "talk about," as in "We need to dialogue about this." Not a good idea.

Elevator pitch. Sometimes called the 60-second pitch. Imagine pitching a concept, idea, or yourself to another person on an elevator between floors. The point is, you have to focus and probably shorten that message.

Go-live date. The day a new product or innovation will be released.

REVIEW: THE SHORT, SHORT VERSION

- Relationship management is a skill. You *can* learn it.
- Leverage your ability to create connections, collaborate, and support others as the foundation for professional relationship building.
- The three stages of relationship management are initiate, cultivate, and maintain.
- Create a diverse personal board of directors to support your career development.

Next, we will examine some of your most important relationships—those with other women in business school.

13

Ladies Who Launch
Building an All-Girls Network

An interviewer once asked me to identify the person who was most influential in my career. I framed a response around my parents because they laid the foundation for who I am personally and professionally. Like most people, afterward I replayed all of the questions, answers, and nuanced details of the interview, but something about that particular question resonated for me. And as I thought/mildly obsessed about it, I began to roll a mental movie of the many people who significantly influenced the professional I had become. Surprisingly, most of the images that came to mind were women. Although I'd spent the early part of my career in the male-dominated financial services industry and overwhelmingly throughout my entire career most of my managers were men, the majority of people who most significantly impacted my professional development, attitude, and trajectory were women. Now, there was an unexpected answer.

ALL-GIRLS NETWORK

In my ideal world, we would not need affinity groups and networks designated for a specific gender or ethnicity. Unfortunately, we are not working in anything that resembles my utopian society. So, this calls for something different, something radical: the all-girls network.

Now, I can imagine what you are saying. "Um, Nicole, your all-girls network sounds a lot like the old-boys network, and why would we want to replicate that?" Well, I'm not suggesting that we want to replicate the reality or the myth of the old-boys network, but let's be honest: they are on to a few things.

The old-boys network is credited with sponsoring other men to help them advance in their careers and with making important connections to facilitate business deals and opportunities. When I think of the old-boys network, I imagine 8 to 10 graying white men in a dimly lit room filled with cigar smoke trading influence and backslapping while draining a bottle of 18-year-old scotch. I'm sure I saw this in a movie, and the image stuck. Peddling influence certainly still exists in business and in politics. Executives are making deals on golf courses or during lunches at exclusive clubs (or maybe even gentlemen's clubs). I'm not sure that will ever go away.

Some guys actually like this. Maybe it makes them feel powerful, like Gordon Gecko from the movie *Wall Street*. As the workforce has diversified, though, the old-boys network has at least gone further underground. More women, minorities, people from different religions and cultures, and progressive men have ascended the professional ranks, which has complicated the hierarchy and the order that once ruled.

I'm sure you would agree that it would be wonderful if the old-boys network disappeared forever. So, you may wonder why I would advocate for an all-girls network. Men think nothing of helping one another be successful, and until we reach that level of entitlement to dole out support as we see fit, then we must be deliberate in our actions. An all-girls network is a bit of a misnomer. I'm not advocating that you have an exclusively female professional network and flush men down the toilet. This in no way is meant to be an exclusionary, cliquey, us-against-them affair. Men have a lot to offer; they run most of the companies and organizations where we want to work, and we need them to be supporters and advocates for women.

The all-girls network is a mind-set that affects the ways we approach, support, and rely on other women. Women with an all-girls network mind-set understand that:

- Having a supportive network of women is important to their professional lives.
- Significantly more women long to be part of an all-girls network than want to go it alone.
- There isn't one right way to engage with other women; only an inclusive attitude is required.
- We don't need to apologize for building strong affiliations based on gender.

The all-girls network is intended to build your confidence as well as your network and to collectively support women in achieving greater career success. With an all-girls network, we gain comfort and confidence in commonality. We have critical mass to address issues and open up new discussions. The all-girls network is a resource, and we can open doors for one another. We each need to have robust professional networks of women not for peddling influence or for shady dealings but instead as the foundation for a long, successful career. Women need camaraderie. Women need role models. Women need support, encouragement, and even a swift kick in the ass sometimes.

Use the 4 Cs to build your all-girls network. As you develop your all-girls network during business school, don't create more work for yourself. You are already cultivating relationships daily, so build your all-girls network in the normal course of business. Start with your first-year section or cohort. Introduce yourself and get to know other women. Be creative as you determine how you can be supportive. Maybe you grab lunch and debrief after class. Or you and another woman visit one of your professors together to get help on a concept with which you are struggling. Beyond the classroom setting, lean on the women's student club on campus for networking events—some will be educational, and others will be completely social. If the women's group pairs second-year students as mentors to first-year students, take advantage of this opportunity—another woman in your all-girls network.

Remember, you don't need to reinvent the wheel. If you are already participating in career-focused student clubs and the career-related events, seek out women there. You might even buddy up during networking events and then share observations and feedback afterward. When I was an investment banking recruiter, I attended a women's event at Chicago Booth. In contrast to the other schools that I visited that fall, the women at Booth were actively including each other in conversations with recruiters, inviting other women into the discussion by introducing them by name. There was an air of inclusivity that was palpable and deliberate. It totally changed the dynamics among the women and with the recruiters.

Nix the cliques. Being inclusive necessarily means breaking up any cliques that form. Business school classes have cliques too. As relationships form, little fiefdoms emerge. It is amazing to me how much of that old high school mentality is still in our psyche. Cliques usually start off in pretty harmless ways. When we enter a new environment, we all tend to gravitate toward certain people—that is, we start to form our own cliques. We do not intend to form an exclusive group and may not even notice that we have done so. We tend to only notice other people's cliques and not our own. We quickly spot the in-crowd of "cool girls" who seem to be hanging out together. We have to break this familiar cycle by being willing to actively engage in relationship building with women who appear to already be in a tight circle of friends. Also think about how you continue to add other women to your group of friends. When you grab lunch or coffee, invite one or two new people. And at events, don't stay huddled with your clique. Open up the circle to encourage others to join in.

Don't expect that with a few small gestures of inclusivity everyone will be friends. We won't all click with one another—no pun intended. In some cases, in fact, it goes beyond not clicking to active dislike. Oh, you know. After a few interactions, there are some women—some *people*—you just don't want to be around and certainly don't want as friends. At this point many of us shut down, avoiding conversations and other interactions with that person.

We learned this behavior in elementary school. I can't tell you how many times I've said, "I just don't like her." That is so fourth grade! There are plenty of guys I don't like either, but there just seems to be a visceral reaction when I don't hit it off with another woman. It is as if friendship was evitable, and when it didn't happen, someone needs to take the blame. It must be her, because it is surely not me. Sound familiar?

It is unfortunate how many MBA alumnae feel as if some of their female classmates were more exclusionary, more cliquey, during business school than their male classmates. We have to break this cycle. It is a disservice to the community of women when we don't support one another and build alliances. We have to rail against this instinctive reaction. We don't all have to be friends. In fact, your professional network should not be centered on friendship, because personal relationships can make thoughtful professional decision making more difficult.

When building relationships in a professional setting, think respect over friendship. If a friendship happens to form, then it is all the better for you and for her. I'm not asking you to ignore your instincts. If you find someone untrustworthy, by all means don't go into business with her, but dismissing her completely as if she has nothing to offer is shortsighted.

When she's not interested. While you may be eager to form relationships, some women aren't interested in having relationships in which the initial connection is gender-based. In business school, they will avoid the women's organization or women-only events. This may be driven by their belief that because they are always working with men in male-dominated environments, there is no reason to deliberately connect with other women. This is a flawed premise, but expect that at least a handful of your female classmates will not see the value in women-only groups—perhaps they have tried them and had a bad experience in the past. Don't force a relationship, and don't take a woman's reluctance as a personal affront to you. Instead, be cordial and remain open to the possibility of a relationship down the road.

PROFESSIONAL-PERSONAL HYBRID RELATIONSHIPS

My eagerness to convince you to pursue professional relationships more deliberately while in business school does not at all reduce the importance of personal relationships you develop. As I did research for this book, I conducted a focus group with six alumnae of Cornell Johnson. The depth of their personal bonds was incredible. They were great friends—they had survived the storm (business school!) together, supporting each other through their various professional and personal challenges and successes. Like the MBA alumnae before you, I hope that you are eager to build relationships with other like-minded women who will support you through the ups and downs of your career and your personal life.

Your relationships don't have to be just personal or just professional. There will be times when you need someone who can relate to your personal desires and goals—someone you're comfortable talking to about the personal yet also understands the professional. This isn't a BFF role. It is a professional contact you can talk to about both your desire to advance in your career and your desire to have a personal life. Michelle Haigh, a graduate of the Wharton School at the University of Pennsylvania, put it best when she said about some of her business school classmates, "They're personally very strong friends, but also you can bounce ideas off them about work or just bitch about work stress in a way that other friends might not relate in the same way."

Of course, there are several men who have been important in my career success. And for most women, as we achieve our career aspirations we will need the support of men at some point along the way—likely at multiple points. But there is something truly special about the relationships that women have with other women. For me, I felt so fortunate each time I made a strong connection with another professional woman. Each time I gained a bit more confidence, knowing that someone else was interested in my success. I also felt more empowered, probably because each positive relationship slowly chipped away at the falsehood that women don't support each other in the workplace. Now, of course I have encountered a few selfish women, but overwhelmingly the women whom I have called colleagues and mentors have been tremendous.

As you go through business school and then reenter the workforce, you will go through ups and downs, you will need support, and you will offer it to others. Your MBA network will include men and women. I encourage you to make a special effort to build relationships and affinity with the women around you. Just as men need time together, so do women.

PROFESSIONAL CONNECTIONS

Women are effective relationship builders, but we often lean aggressively toward building personal relationships over professional ones. This was no more evident than in my conversations with MBA alumnae as I was writing this book. Women MBAs spoke of finding lasting personal friendships among their business school peers but not equally developing powerful professional relationships among their classmates. This is alarming! Many women MBAs did not cultivate enduring, lucrative professional connections with their classmates and thus did not unlock arguably the most valuable aspect of the MBA program: relationships.

I don't want to oversimplify this. Women MBAs are savvy and have developed professional relationships through other sources, namely in their post-MBA organizations. But not fully exploiting the unique relationship-building environment of business school is a missed opportunity. Business school is rife with professional contacts that women can leverage throughout their careers, and all too often we are not availing ourselves of these door-opening relationships. Your MBA program will provide a forum for building strong professional relationships with other women, including classmates, professors, administrators, alumni, and other professionals.

Take full advantage of business school to develop relationships for your personal board of directors, which we discussed in Chapter 12. Also, consider how you will develop a well-rounded professional community of women. There are several roles that women can play as you navigate the internship and full-time job search and in helping you to be successful once you are in the positions. Here are some of the cast of characters you will need to gather:

- *Accountability partners.* Two to three women in your class who have similar professional aspirations and are recruiting for the same industry. Accountability partners will hold you accountable for goals and tasks that you set for yourself. And they will have your back during the recruiting process—possibly sharing job opportunities that they hear about or giving you their notes from the strategy class that you missed when you had an interview.

- *Industry peers.* Women at your level who are in the same or a related industry and provide the basis for your industry network. Industry peers will include your accountability partners and also the other first-year women who are pursuing or previously worked in your industry of interest as well as second-year students who may have done their summer internship in the industry. Not only will you actively network with this group while on campus, but expect that you will directly or indirectly work with them professionally for years to come.

- *Industry insiders.* Women who are slightly more senior to you in the same or a related industry. Industry insiders provide guidance on navigating the search process and the industry environment and can make introductions to other industry professionals. Your industry insiders are women who attended business school two to four years before you.
- *Mentors.* Women who are much more senior to you in the same or a related industry and who provide guidance or direct support in advancing your career. Your mentors will be alumni and corporate executives who may or may not be within the company you intern with or work for. Mentors are key to career success. Studies show that women with mentors are more likely to start in higher professional positions.
- *Sponsors and backers.* Your sponsors will work at the company where you are employed, and they will choose to actively advocate on your behalf. That's right. You don't choose them; they choose you. You don't generally have sponsors outside of a work context, so you won't have them while in business school. You will have women backers who have a positive professional impression of you and will recommend or support you if called on. Your backers will be fellow classmates and professors. They have strong professional reputations, and you may call on them when changing industries and/or when you need introductions to people in their networks.

These are not simply roles that can be played by women, if you happen to identify one. You should intentionally engage women in these important support positions, particularly industry insiders and mentors, as they can help you avoid pitfalls and identify opportunities. You can't go through every experience, nor would you want to. While each woman responds differently to situations, there is something that profoundly resonates when you have other women you can consult who have experienced challenges and successes that you may be facing.

You may already have women who serve some of these roles in your professional life. Take stock of your relationships and then begin to fill in the gaps. While you will cultivate accountability partners and industry peers, expect that most women within your MBA network won't serve an immediate purpose as it relates to the roles outlined above. Instead, these will be relationships to foster and maintain for affinity and for future use. We need each other, or at least most of us do. I am suggesting that you deliberately build a community of women that is professional, supportive, and personally empowering.

JARGON ALERT

Holistic approach. A well-rounded way of addressing something.

Next Gen. Or next generation. An improved or revamped product or service.

Organic. A fresh or basic approach. Often used to describe something that develops without deliberate cultivation or action.

REVIEW: THE SHORT, SHORT VERSION

- An all-girls network can benefit you in a number of ways. It is not intended to be the female version of the dreaded old-boys network.
- Break down your all-girls network into accountability partners, industry peers, industry insiders, mentors and sponsors, and backers.
- Be sure to include hybrid relationships whereby you can discuss your personal as well as professional goals.
- Support other women. No more cliques. Be inclusive.

We have covered almost every possible relationship that you will have in business school—except one. For our next chapter, it is time for an honest look at dating.

14

Manhandle
Locking Up Mr. Right, 2.5 Kids, and Fido

The MRS degree—going to school and leaving with a husband. A sexist concept of the past, right? Well, we don't talk about the MRS degree in polite circles, particularly not polite business school circles. MBA women are ambitious, talented, career-minded women, and business school is about advancing your career, not about getting hitched. I completely agree with that premise. At the same time, though, I acknowledge that MBA students are attending business school in prime marrying years. Besides, if you want to be a CEO, we would certainly talk about how to achieve that professional goal. In the same way, if you want to be married, we should talk about how to achieve that personal goal.

TO DATE OR NOT TO DATE

Regardless of how you prioritize dating and finding a significant other, if you have any inclination to date in business school, you must understand the potential pitfalls and avoid missteps. Every MBA has dating war stories of classmates who did boneheaded things on the dating scene—guys dating multiple women, very public hookups, or very public breakups. The very worst are the married students who act like single students. No need to spend time on that. Suffice it to say, stay clear of married men who are trying to relive their single years.

If you don't date, don't hate. We all have our priorities. You might want to read this chapter anyway in case you change your mind.

If you do date, here are the ground rules.

1. No drunken hookups (or sober ones for that matter). Sex and business don't mix. You may have needs, but find someplace other than your classmates (or administrators or faculty) to fulfill those needs. Never forget that your business school community is your primary professional network. Your reputation within this community is too important for random hookups.

2. If your primary goal in going to business school is the MRS degree and you rate immediately acquiring a husband higher than developing your career, I strongly encourage you to reprioritize or consider skipping business school altogether. In my opinion, you would be better off staying gainfully employed, avoiding the expense of business school, and joining match.com or eharmony.com.

3. Respect the fact that women in your class have different priorities, and try to reserve judgment. So much easier said than done! Your classmates will prioritize finding a significant other in business school differently. Remember that we have our own goals, but we also internalize differently the crazy societal and familial pressure surrounding marriage. Some women have a tough time holding their mothers' wedding planning at bay.

4. A woman on the prowl never gets the guy. This is a universal dating principle, or at least it should be. The quickest way to drive men away is to chase them. Guys have a sixth sense for MRS seekers. Just kidding—men are generally pretty oblivious and unaware. It is just that a desperate woman is that transparent. In a survey that I conducted of MBA alumnae who met their husbands in business school, the majority said that finding a spouse during business school was not important to them. No chasing!

I am not the Millionaire Matchmaker, though over the last 15 years I have seen hundreds of relationships start and stop or continue to marriage. I can't guarantee that you will find your spouse in business school, but there are a few things that you can do to best position yourself for the dual MBA/MRS degree. You must understand the environment, be clear about who you are and what you want, and then act accordingly.

UNDERSTANDING THE ENVIRONMENT

Understand the business school environment. Don't underestimate this step. As we discussed early on, business school is more like high school than college. Even the larger schools are pretty small by universal school standards. It is an intimate environment in which there truly is a community, and this enables you to bond with more of your classmates and develop enduring professional and personal relationships. The environment created is an overwhelmingly positive one, though at times it can be cliquey and gossipy.

If you are actively involved in community activities and spend time on campus (which is often just one building), you will see who is spending time together and the cliques that form. Many of these affinities are not intentional but instead are circumstantial and based on section or cohort, career interest, ethnicity, or national origin. Add alcohol and sleep deprivation to spending entirely too much time together, and gossip is a virtual certainty. This environment may make it more difficult to keep a relationship out of the public eye. It also increases the likelihood that you see the person you are dating all of the time, which may be a little awkward early in a relationship.

The small size of the business school community also leads to a unified social and professional life. If you were working in a major city before attending business school, your personal and social life was quite likely separate from your professional life. You could be pretty confident that you weren't going to see your manager or coworkers on a Friday night. This does not hold true in business school, particularly if you are going to school outside of a large city such as New York or Los Angeles. It is hard to separate your social and professional lives in business school.

In business school, relationships can be accelerated because students are seeing each other so frequently. There is nothing inherently wrong with this. One alumna I spoke with met her husband during orientation before school started. She had determined that she would not date in school, but her future husband was persistent. It worked out for them, but this acceleration can make it harder to casually date if you are not looking for a serious relationship. It can also make ending a relationship more difficult.

The most important thing to remember when dating is that breaking up really is hard to do. Sometimes breakups are mutual and easy, but usually one person has stronger feelings than the other and gets hurt. This pain can be exacerbated by having to see each other in the normal course of the school day and by having to see the other person dating someone else. Even if you were the one who broke it off, it still sucks to see him cuddled up with one of your classmates. Breakups can also lead to unwanted gossip as others try to piece together what actually happened between the two of you. Business school breakups can be so dramatic that many MBA alumnae suggest that you avoid dating in business school altogether. I don't take such a hard line, but I do encourage you to proceed with some caution.

Okay, I'm going to say this more than once, so pay attention, please. Avoid dating someone in your section or cohort during your first year.

Imagine sitting in your first-year section in the second row of a U-shaped room, and directly across is your Adonis. He's gorgeous, and you hang on his every word in class. He looks back at you longingly, and a romance ensues. After a short period of bliss, you determine that your Adonis is a bit of a windbag, and the sparks fly—out the door. But your section assignment is set, so you have to see and hear him every day for another eight months. To add insult to injury, Adonis is now dating a woman who sits directly behind you, so he's gazing in your direction but not at you.

At a number of schools, you take all of your core classes with the same cohort or section. You spend hours together. This is your first layer of relationship building. Avoid creating an uncomfortable situation by dating someone who is in your section. If you feel like he is really the one, your soul mate, he will still be the one after your first year! If you must date someone in the section, take it very slowly. Discretion on both of your parts is essential. No goo-goo eyes in class!

THE MEN

Business schools have 25–35 percent women. Some schools recently crossed the 40 percent threshold, so we are getting closer to gender parity. Although there is no public data on marital status by gender, all would agree that men are more likely to be married than their female counterparts. This is driven by age (men attend business school at an older average age than women) and relationship dynamics (married women are more reluctant to pursue full-time MBA programs). As the saying goes, the odds are good, but the goods are odd. Although men significantly outnumber women in business school, after accounting for the married ones, the near-married ones (engaged or almost engaged), and the downright strange ones, the pickings aren't as good as the overall numbers might suggest. This might yield more competition among the women for the superstar men. With that said, on average business school does offer a solid pool of men.

Thank the admissions team for recruiting high-achieving, successful young men to your business school! And these days most business schools also conduct background checks, so you can be confident that there are no felons or criminals in the bunch. Every business school class has its pompous men roaming the halls; they are often associated with the investment bankers. I can't argue that there were more than a few tools in my class who were aspiring bankers, yet at the same time some of the most awesome, eligible men in my class were also headed to Wall Street.

ATTRACTING THE RIGHT GUY FOR YOU

Know yourself and what you want. While it is critical to understand the business school environment and the dating landscape, equally important is to know yourself and what you want. It is all right to determine that you won't date classmates (there are other grad programs!) or at least that you won't date them during your first year or until after graduation.

What are you looking for in a man? You might want to write it out. What are your requirements, those must-have qualities that you won't compromise on? A productive citizen or gainfully employed? Certain religious affiliation or political views? Don't be too rigid, but be honest with yourself about what you want. Along with your requirements, consider the optional nice-to-have qualities that you would like in a man. I had hoped to find a man who was a bit more domestic than my husband turned out to be. I can cook and clean but am not a huge fan, so I thought that it would be efficient to have a husband who enjoyed those things. Alas, my husband is less of a fan than I am. This wasn't a deal breaker for me, but it did mean that he needed to get comfortable with maid service and eating out more than the average couple.

I'm all for planning, but there is absolutely no reason to agonize over how husband and children fit with your career when there is no current prospect of a husband. Don't get ahead of yourself. Also, this speculation will make you crazy. And crazy women attract crazy men!

Women (and men for that matter) spend lots of time listing what they want in a mate but not enough time on themselves. What are you bringing to the table—the good, the bad, and the ugly? It is important that you take a personal inventory. Be honest about your baggage. If you have deep-seated issues with men, now is the time to deal with them, not later when you are actually in a relationship. Look inward, but don't be overly critical. We all have our issues and room for improvement. Successful dating requires self-acceptance. Being overly self-critical is not attractive.

ACT ACCORDING TO THE ENVIRONMENT
AND WHAT YOU WANT

After you have given thought to what you want and what you bring to the table, take a look at your personal brand. As you now know, your brand is not about show or surface but instead is about developing your core strengths and then ensuring that the vibes you give off are consistent with who you are. I'm outgoing and gregarious, and I couldn't be demure if you paid me. Coy and reserved are not attributes that should be on my list.

Even if I was able to fake it for a little while, my husband would have been duped when he found out that I was an excessive talker. Develop a personal brand that will endure beyond your two years in school. Keep it consistent, and this means keeping it real.

Don't be frustrated if the perfect man doesn't appear instantly. Mr. Right may not be in the halls of your business school. He may be a friend of one of your classmates or of a future coworker. Take a long-term view of dating. It is not an instant-gratification pursuit. In the meantime, get involved with and meet a lot of people. Now, I hope I've made a compelling argument against dating your section mate during the first year. That still leaves lots of people.

Consider joining team-oriented and social clubs. Your section mates should be off-limits for dating prospects, so look instead to campus clubs that are team-oriented or social in nature. You don't have to be a jock or a connoisseur to participate. I would suggest that you have some interest in the actual activities. Man-hunting within the club does not count as an interest! To give you an example of clubs that might facilitate interaction with first- and second-year men, consider the University of Southern California Marshall School of Business, which has social and athletic clubs such as the Marshall Wine & Beer Club, the Marshall Outdoor Club, and the Art Society at Marshall. Ultimately, your best dating prospects will be men with whom you have things in common, so pursuing your own interests will facilitate meeting men with higher compatibility.

Participate in activities that facilitate conversation. In order to date someone, you need to know something about him, and it is much easier if you can actually talk to each other. Lectures and films are fine—for later. For now, find opportunities to converse.

Okay, this is totally random, but it is my book, so I can say what I want! Can we let go of the stilettos and skirts that are too short? This is not consistent with a professional woman's brand. And if you must rock the high heels, could you learn to walk in them? Nothing says unsexy like a woman who can't walk in heels. Better to strut your stuff in a pair of ballet slipper flats. You have to figure out what works for you, but personal brand is about walking the walk in or out of stilettos. I feel better now that I shared that.

MAINTAINING YOUR RELATIONSHIP IN BUSINESS SCHOOL

Dating another MBA student will complicate your community building experience. It is no less challenging, though, if you have a significant other, particularly if your spouse or boyfriend (or girlfriend) is not a student. You will have to integrate your relationship into your new business school life.

Significant others are an important source of support when business school gets really stressful, and for most couples business school is just another experience in the relationship—not good, not bad. Just know that business school will exacerbate any problems you already have. If you have relationship issues before business school, expect them to get worse. Business school is not the place to try to fix your relationship or save your marriage. If you have problems, try to address them before school.

The reality is that not every woman arrives on campus young, single, and ready to mingle. Some women are actually married or in a serious relationship, a few with their significant other in tow, but most leave their significant others in another city or state. It can be really difficult to move away and embark on this new MBA journey with that person still in your old world.

It didn't quite work for me. I didn't leave my boyfriend in another state; I left him in the next building, the law school where I had been the year before. No regrets. He wasn't actually the one, but I can tell you that it was really difficult to maintain a relationship with someone outside of the business school. So many first-year students struggle with this, particularly in the first semester of the first year. Business school can be overwhelming in the first semester, and as you acclimate it will seem as if you spend every minute of every day thinking, talking, networking, eating, and sleeping business school.

On the one hand, having the opportunity to decompress with someone not associated with business school can be a welcome break from the business school insanity, but on the other hand, it is hard to get on the phone after a day full of classes, meeting with your study group, and club activities. Fifteen or 20 minutes seems wholly inadequate for summarizing everything that went on in your day and try to give context and background so that the story makes sense, all so that you can vent and also help your significant other become part of your life. And, oh wait, he actually should be able to get a word in about what's going on with him and his job and life.

Communication. Business school can be a stressful and busy time, and communication is the key to making it through this period with your relationship intact. This is not meant to be the guide to relationship success but instead focuses on how to minimize the negative impact of business school on your relationship and vice versa.

To maintain your relationship, set aside quality time for your cutie. There is no substitute for time and being present with one another. The phone is your friend. As your workload increases and activities abound, try to honor your quality time and space. I mentioned that my relationship in my first year didn't work. Well, second time's the charm. My relationship with my husband got serious when he was a first-year student in business school. On weekdays, we would talk every day before he met with his study group for 20 to 30 minutes; when he was really busy, maybe it was only 10 minutes. Of course, when we could we would check in more often, such as during the day or after learning team at 11:00 or later at night, but we talked every day. I was much better prepared to be a business school partner (partner to a business school student) because I had been through the first-year experience, so I could really empathize with the workload and the stress. A partner who is a fellow MBA student or an MBA graduate understands what you are going through.

Quality time. Quality time with your significant other will improve your sanity (it will be nice to talk with someone about something other than business school) and will help you maintain your relationship. Quality time will likely be more important for your significant other than for you. You have the big life change. You are in business school, and he is leading the same life as before. You will be so busy with course work, club and social activities, and career search that for most of the day you won't miss your significant other. You frankly just won't have the time or the brain space. If you are in a new city, you won't have constant reminders of him. For your significant other, though, it may be a different story. He is still in the city that you left, he is still living in the same apartment where you hung out all of the time and passing the restaurants where you once ate. He will find that there are many more voids or reminders that you aren't there than what you are experiencing. Difficult as this may be to accept, although this may be the best and most exciting time of your life, it may not be the best time in your partner's life.

Be mindful of how your business school move may impact him. The best solution for filling the voids is to see each other in person. Sometimes you just need a hug! As early as possible, schedule when you are going to visit him and when he is coming to campus to visit you. This will give you something to look forward to. I'm particularly a fan of getting him to campus, as it will enable him to meet your classmates and your friends. This will give him context for your phone conversations so he can stay up on the drama and excitement of school. His visits to campus will really help you integrate your life with him and your business school life.

Remember that talking and communicating are two different things. You don't have to have deep, emotional conversations every time you talk, but periodically you must delve into tough talk such as setting expectations and sharing feelings. It may be hard for him to understand why you are so stressed out. I mean, you're in school. Before you were working 40-plus hours, and now you only have class for 15 hours a week. What's the big deal? With business school you have to experience it to really understand it, so don't be too hard on him if he doesn't quite get it. Try not to take your stress out on your significant other. At the same time, don't pretend for his sake that you aren't stressed. Let him support you.

Finally, if you are bringing your significant other to business school with you, the same rules apply. Communicate your expectations and set aside quality time. You don't need to travel to see each other, but creating opportunities for one-on-one time is still important. Whether a date night or a weekend getaway, make time for one another. It can be hard for your significant other to uproot his life and join the business school community as a partner. Some men resist being a school partner. Many MBA programs have partner organizations, such as Stanford BizPartners. Columbia Business School's Better Halves helps new residents find their way around New York City and creates events for significant others, fiancées/fiancés, spouses, and families of students to meet one another. The partner organizations on business school campuses are largely women, spouses of the men in your class, and so it can be hard for your beau to get engaged. Be understanding about how this might be a challenge for him, and at the same time share what you are going through.

SOME WAYS TO KEEP A MAN

Address your issues. As you take stock of what you are bringing to the table, address or at least acknowledge your issues. If you tend to be possessive in relationships, it might be useful to uncover the cause of your controlling behavior. You may not be able to immediately change it, but you can certainly be more cognizant of it. There are certain issues and situations that require a professional (a counselor or psychologist). Don't be afraid to seek out an independent third party to talk it through. There is a stigma about counseling that causes many people to avoid it. Your friends can't help you with everything. Sometimes you need an objective perspective.

Keep it drama-free. Do you have friends who always have drama? If you don't, then you are likely the friend with the drama. She tends to find herself in sticky situations, and when there isn't anything, she can create it. Drama-free is a good general strategy but particularly when mixing personal and professional relationships in business school. Keeping a strong reputation is your top priority, so act with the highest level of integrity. There is nothing wrong with a little mystery and intrigue in a relationship, but avoid misleading behavior.

Find the balance. Some women are not good daters. Dating by definition requires taking it one date at a time. These women are instead serial girlfriends. After the first date they basically go to girlfriend mode, even if their dates haven't actually become their boyfriends. They turn into instant wifey, cooking his meals and spending every free moment of the day and night at his place. This translates to clingy, a condition that most people are allergic to. If you suspect that you are a serial girlfriend, be careful not to move the relationship forward too quickly. Don't forget that you have a life.

Take your time. Imagine walking into orientation and there are, say, 50 single men. Regardless of the number of women, there is reason to be excited. Those are some serious prospects that could have you licking your chops thinking about where you should begin. I mean, you are an ambitious, take-charge woman in business school! Easy, sparky! Instead, let it come to you. Get the lay of the land; see what's out there first. When you are open to dating, that energy is emitted into the universe. Let it hang in the air a little. There is no need to thrust yourself onto the dating scene too quickly. When the suitors do start calling, continue to take your time. Don't let a persistent man rush you.

Mixed emotions send mixed signals. Imagine that you start dating someone. Everything is going well, and you think there is long-term potential for this relationship. He's looking at jobs in New York, and you don't know if you should start looking for jobs there also. I mean, if you are going to get serious, you shouldn't move to the other side of the country, right? So you start pushing him to characterize the relationship and share his intentions and timeline. Pump the brakes! Slow down! You have to figure out how to communicate effectively with one another to determine if you will consider each other in your plans, but avoid false urgency. Also, know that if the relationship has long-term potential, he's likely thinking about it too.

Stay focused on your primary goal. Business school is career school, not MRS school. Even in the midst of yummy good times, a great social life, and dating, remember that these are all superfluous benefits. Your primary purpose is advancing your career. Figure out how you keep that in the top of your mind. A quote on your mirror that you see every morning? A reminder in your calendar to keep your eye on the ball? Do what it takes to remain focused.

Use early events to build professional relationships and friendships, not to peruse the dating prospects.

Be yourself. Temper behavior that increases the likelihood of disastrous dating or relationships. But in the process of being a good dater, don't lose yourself. My hope is that you find someone who likes you and supports you, quirks and all. You have to be yourself so he can get to know you.

Most MBA students come to campus single and leave single—although in every class there are at least a handful of students who will meet and marry another student. This is the exception and not the rule, however. I'm a fan of dating in business school, but it is not for everyone. If you are looking for a serious relationship, consider one MBA alumna's advice: "Find the smart quiet guy who is confident but not cocky and who isn't trying to date as many women as possible in B-school." Good luck!

JARGON ALERT

Drinking the Kool-Aid. Believing whatever one is told; naive. A reference to the 1978 Jonestown Massacre.

Face time. Required physical presence. A way of communicating in person that does not involve the telephone or the Internet. Interestingly, Apple has co-opted the word to brand its videotelephony, which enables you to video chat without being in the same physical space.

Leapfrog. Attempting to jump ahead of the competition by undertaking a major change that may or may not prove disastrous.

REVIEW: THE SHORT, SHORT VERSION

- Do not date anyone in your section or cohort during your first year.
- Understand your environment, and know that it is close to impossible to keep your personal and professional lives separate.
- Remember that you are in business school to get an MBA first. If the MRS degree is more important, reconsider your decision to attend business school.
- If you do begin dating someone and he has not committed, do not turn into instant wifey.
- If you are already in a relationship when you arrive at business school, ensure that it is a healthy one. If you have major issues before business school, assume that they may get worse while you are in business school.
- Create opportunities for one-on-one time with your significant other.
- And, once again, do *not* date anyone in your section or cohort during your first year.

15

Catapulted
Putting It All Together

As you have probably figured out, you can't read this book a week before school and implement everything. Maybe you're thinking, *How am I going to build relationships if I don't have a personal brand? How can I leverage something I haven't even identified yet? What if I don't know exactly what I want to do or who I want to become? Am I ready for business school if my aspirations aren't clear?* Stop! I don't want you to read this book and freak out. I want you to be excited about business school and confident in your ability to maximize the experience. If you do even 30 percent of what I have suggested, you *will* catapult your career, I promise.

You can't do everything, nor should you try. Establish the outcomes that you want to achieve and from there determine the most effective approach to your classroom experience, club engagement, career exploration, and community and social life. Create a plan with your own personal checklist. This book offers many examples that you can employ, but you have to decide what will work best for you. While what you do is important, how you think is the true driver of your success. If you take nothing else from this book, know that your mind-set will propel your actions. Your belief in your abilities and your determination to leverage your MBA slingshot will carry you further than racing to tick off your business school to-do list.

You will have an incredible experience in business school. You will learn more than you ever imagined you could. You will build lifelong relationships. You will develop into an even more effective, capable professional. And you will have fun! Of course, business school will not be without its challenges. For most students, the first year of business school brings tremendous stress, from challenging course work, club activities, and speakers almost daily to the seemingly endless job search and the social activities, including happy hours, parties, and school traditions, however crazy. And this doesn't even take into account nonschool activities, including family, significant others, and other obligations.

When we're stressed out, it can be hard to step out of the situation and objectively evaluate what is causing our stress and how to address it. We're overwhelmed and in the midst of freaking out. At that moment, it can seem impossible to figure out the real issues, but it is exactly at that time, in the middle of the anxiety, that you have to take control. You have to remind yourself that stress is as much a part of the business school experience as first-year finance. It is like a business school initiation. Everyone has to go through it. When your anxiety level goes up, try to defuse it as much as possible, but accept that feeling a little stressed is normal.

As with most stressful situations, along the business school journey you have to take a step back to appreciate where you are and evaluate how you will move forward. Once you are on campus, it is going to feel like time is moving at warp speed. On some days, you may feel like you don't even have time for a bathroom break, let alone an hour to sit quietly and reflect. Make time during your business school experience to consider what is working, what is not, what you learned about yourself, and what you will do differently going forward. Has the experience changed your ego and aspirations? Did it highlight additional skills that you want to build or experiences that you want to have? Did you achieve something that a year ago you thought was impossible?

Business school is going to stretch your abilities and challenge your thinking. One day you will make a great comment in class or get elected to a club leadership position, and you will be on top of the world. And then, just like that, the next day you won't get selected to interview with your top-choice company or won't get the grade you wanted on a test, and you will be back to doubting yourself. Through the ups and downs of business school (and frankly beyond), you must remember that you have within you everything you need to be successful. You are authentically you, and that is enough.

Throughout the book, I have been emphatic about the importance of professional relationships and the opportunity that business school presents to you for developing those connections. Relationship building at its core is really just about convincing other people that they should support you and your career advancement—that they should invest in the real you. If you believe that you are worth the investment, others will too.

Relationships, along with the skills and knowledge that you develop in business school, enable you to harness who you are to get what you want. This is why I want you to keep going back to Chapter 3 to ground yourself in your ego—in who you are. As you remain focused on who you are and who you want to become, you are going to live authentically. You will have confidence in the career and life paths that fit you even as your classmates are doing something else. Your first impulse won't be to ask "What is everyone else doing?" It will be "What do I want to do?"

Catapulting your career depends on moving toward who you are and what you want to become. Ambitious people don't really *reach* their ultimate goals. We are always *in search of* them. Once we near them, we may hit an intermediate milestone, but then our vision expands and we can see beyond where we thought we were headed. The bigger goal was always there, but our eyes weren't able to focus that far and wide.

Use this book to help you build knowledge, enhance your skills, and develop relationships in business school, not to make you someone else but to make you a better you.

Now is the time! Don't just talk about it, be about it! Today is the day that you are going to unabashedly and unapologetically go for what you want! As women, we deserve to get what we want. Think about that. Do you believe that you deserve to get what you want? We can have another conversation about whether the sacrifice to get what you want is worth it or not. I'm not interested in that right here. I'm referring to the inherent value that you place on yourself. You can sit on your couch and eat bonbons every day, have deep self-worth, and believe that you are entitled to enjoy those treats.

On the other hand, you could be running the largest nonprofit organization, helping millions of people, and feel that you are an imposter, not deserving the success that you've had. Too many women in business school and in other places where successful women dwell are like the second woman who feels like a fraud. As much as they are striving for more, they are questioning their worth and the significance of their goals, desires, and aspirations.

Self-doubt leads to lack of confidence, which then causes us to look for permission to act and to even exist. We seek permission to validate who we are. Just consider the MBA classroom. Self-doubt leads us to seek permission to participate in the discussion. We open our comments asking permission. "Can I add a thought to the conversation?" We seek permission by overpreparing for class, putting in extra hours to have some confidence that we are capable of making a cogent statement. You are a student in the class just like anyone else. You raised your hand like anyone else. You don't need permission from someone else to share your opinion. Forget permission! What's the saying? "It's better to beg for forgiveness than ask for permission." Instead of asking permission, demonstrate your entitlement to do, accomplish, and be anything you choose.

Just as we deserve the space to be authentically who we are, it is our right to test new things too. We women are entitled to fail, to take risks, and, most important, to dream without the limits that others have put on us as well as the limits that we put on ourselves. We are so conditioned that all too frequently, we don't even dream big. At one point when I was running a nonprofit, it hit me that I had basically accomplished everything that I had set out to do in that position. You might think that I would be excited about the achievements and the accolades, but I was devastated. In that moment, it dawned on me that I had stopped dreaming in favor of planning these realistic aspirations that I knew I could achieve. I had created these bite-size, not-too-tough goals that would always make me look good, knowing that I basically couldn't fail. Is that what my talent and capability had come down to? Not failing? In essence, by not failing I was failing to dream, not moving toward everything I was truly put on Earth to achieve.

Replace self-doubt with confidence. Replace permission with entitlement. Look yourself in the mirror every morning and say, "I deserve to be successful, I deserve to dream. Today is the day." Trust that even with the biggest seemingly impossible dream, you can't be held back. That dream will catapult you forward.

Notes

INTRODUCTION

1. "U.S. Women in Business: Pyramid," Catalyst, July 1, 2013, http://www .catalyst.org/knowledge/us-women-business-0.
2. Bureau of Labor Statistics, U.S. Department of Labor, "Changes in Women's Labor Force Participation in the 20th Century," February 16, 2000, http://www.bls.gov/opub/ted/2000/feb/wk3/art03.htm.
3. National Center for Education Statistics, U.S. Department of Education, "Table 247: Earned Degrees Conferred by Degree-Granting Institutions, by Level of Degree and Sex of Student; Selected Years, 1869–70 to 2013–14," http://nces.ed.gov/programs/digest/d04/tables/dt04_247.asp.
4. "History: 1972," The Washington Post Company, http://www.washpostco .com/phoenix.zhtml?c=62487&p=irol-history1950.
5. Nicole Lindsay, *MBAdvantage: Diversity Outreach Benchmarking Report* (Stamford, CT: Strong Seed Publishing, 2013).
6. "Quick Take: Women MBAs," Catalyst, http://www.catalyst.org/ knowledge/women-mbas.

CHAPTER 1

1. Graduate Management Admissions Council, "Profile of Graduate Management Admission Test Candidates, 2012–2013: Executive Summary," 2013, http://www.gmac.com/~/media/Files/gmac/Research/GMAT%20 Test%20Taker%20Data/2013-gmat-profile-exec-summary.pdf.
2. Nancy M. Carter and Christine Silva, "Pipeline's Broken Promise," Catalyst, 2010, http://www.catalyst.org/knowledge/pipelines-broken-promise.

3. Matt Separa, "Infographic: The Gender Pay Gap," Center for American Progress, April 16, 2012, http://www.americanprogress.org/issues/women/news/2012/04/16/11435/infographic-the-gender-pay-gap/.

4. Carter and Silva, "Pipeline's Broken Promise."

5. Ibid.

6. Christine Silva, Nancy M. Carter, and Anna Beninger, "Good Intentions, Imperfect Execution? Women Get Fewer of the 'Hot Jobs' Needed to Advance," Catalyst, 2012, http://www.catalyst.org/knowledge/good-intentions -imperfect-execution-women-get-fewer-hot-jobs-needed -advance.

7. Catalyst Research Staff, Carol Hollenshead, and Jeanne Wilt, "Women and the MBA: Gateway to Opportunity," Catalyst, 2000, http://www .catalyst.org/knowledge/women-and-mba-gateway-opportunity.

8. Harvard Business School, "Life & Leadership after HBS: A Preview of Findings," April 2013, http://www.hbs.edu/women50/images/women _survey_preview_130402.pdf. See also Lauren Everitt, "Leaning Elsewhere: Are Harvard B-School Women Opting Out?," CNN Money, April 12, 2013, http://management.fortune.cnn.com/2013/04/12/harvard -mba-women-careers-motherhood/.

CHAPTER 4

1. Lauren Ready, "Taking Charge: A Roadmap for a Successful Career and a Meaningful Life for High Potential Corporate Women Leaders," ICEDR Special Report, 2012, http://www.icedr.org/research/documents/ICEDRSpecialReport-TakingCharge_000.pdf.

CHAPTER 10

1. "Are Women Investors Hard-Hearted? Why Women Expect More Than Men from Financial Services Firms and What They Want," Hearts & Wallets, http://heartsandwallets.com/are-women-investors-hard-hearted/news/2012/02/.

CHAPTER 11

1. Joe Hadfield, "Women Speak Less When They're Outnumbered," EurekAlert, September 18, 2018, http://www.eurekalert.org/pub _releases/2012-09/byu-wsl091812.php.

CHAPTER 12

1. "Madeleine Albright on Barriers Broken and Barriers That Remain," *Wall Street Journal,* May 7, 2012, http://online.wsj.com/news/articles/SB10001424052702304746604577383721974234282.

Suggested Resources

ORGANIZATIONS

85 Broads, www.85broads.com
Black MBA Women, www.blackmbawomen.com
Catalyst, www.catalyst.org
Diversity MBA Prep, www.diversitymbaprep.com
Forté Foundation, www.fortefoundation.org
MBA Women International, www.mbawomen.org

BOOKS

Babcock, Linda, and Sara Laschever. *Women Don't Ask: The High Cost of Avoiding Negotiation—and Positive Strategies for Change.* New York: Bantam, 2007.

Collins, James C., and Jerry I. Porras. *Built to Last: Successful Habits of Visionary Companies.* New York: HarperCollins, 2002.

Frankel, Lois. *Nice Girls Don't Get the Corner Office: 101 Unconscious Mistakes Women Make That Sabotage Their Careers.* New York: Business Plus, 2004.

Hadary, Sharon, and Laura Henderson. *How Women Lead: The Essential Strategies Successful Women Know.* New York: McGraw-Hill, 2012.

Hewlett, Sylvia Ann. *Forget a Mentor, Find a Sponsor: The New Way to Fast-Track Your Career.* Boston: Harvard Business Review Press, 2013.

Monosoff, Tamara. *Your Million Dollar Dream.* New York: McGraw-Hill, 2010.

Rezvani, Selena. *Pushback: How Smart Women Ask—and Stand Up—for What They Want.* San Francisco: Jossey-Bass, 2012.

Sandberg, Sheryl. *Lean In: Women, Work, and the Will to Lead.* New York: Knopf, 2013.

Shuchart, Carrie, and Chris Ryan. *Case Studies & Cocktails: The "Now What?" Guide to Surviving Business School.* New York: Manhattan Prep Publishing, 2011.

Steven Silbiger, *The Ten-Day MBA: A Step-by-Step Guide to Mastering the Skills Taught in America's Top Business Schools.* New York: HarperCollins, 2012.

Thakor, Manisha, and Sharon Kedar. *On My Own Two Feet: A Modern Girl's Guide to Personal Finance.* Avon, MA: Adams Media, 2007.

Index

About the Author

Nicole M. Lindsay is a career and leadership development expert. Lindsay earned her BS from the University of Connecticut and her JD/MBA from the University of Virginia and has served as a former MBA admissions officer, corporate MBA recruiter, and nonprofit executive. She currently directs leadership development efforts at a Connecticut foundation. Lindsay is the founder of DiversityMBAPrep, the only online community that provides MBA admissions coaching resources for women and minorities, and is the author of *MBAdvantage: Diversity Outreach Benchmarking Report* (2013). Lindsay serves on the University of Virginia Darden School Alumni Board and the Board of Directors of the New York Chapter of the UConn Alumni Association. She is the recipient of the 2011 University of Connecticut Honors Program Distinguished Alumna Award. Lindsay has been featured in CNN's *Black in America II, U.S. News & World Report,* TheDailyMuse.com, Lifehacker.com, and Forbes.com. She is licensed to practice law in Connecticut and Georgia. Follow Lindsay on Twitter at @MBAMinority.